GUILTY!

Keeping God's Covenant of Love with Israel

By Dr. James and Patty Hutchens
Chaplain (Brigadier General) U. S. Army (Ret.)

*To Linda Morris —
With best wishes for
God's richest blessings.
Jim & Pat Hutchens*

JER 29:11

Guilty!
by Jim and Patty Hutchens

For information contact:
The Jerusalem Connection
PO Box 20295
Washington, DC 20041
Phone: 703-707-0014
Email: HutchensJM@aol.com

Printed in the United States of America

ISBN 1-594679-16-9

www.xulonpress.com

Dedication

To all who love Israel,
To the One who said,
"I will most assuredly plant them in this Land,
with all my heart and soul."

To all who are in the midst of hardship,
struggle, disappointment or rejection,
His grace *is* sufficient.
No matter how many promises God has made,
they are all "*Yes*" in Jesus Christ.

Acknowledgements

Without the faithfulness of our God
And the steadfast love of our children,
Matt, Sarah and Rachel,
multiplied now in their beautiful families,
"Guilty" could have had a tragic end,
rather than a glorious victory.

Special Thanks

To Dr. Larry Keefauver, editor and motivator par excel lance,
To Mali Terrel, re-editor with compassion for the cause.
To Dave Hail, the greatest of God's idea men.

ENDORSEMENT

Dr. and Mrs. James Hutchens
PO Box 20295
Washington, DC 20041

Dear Jim and Patty:

Thank you for sharing your manuscript with me. Given the painful experience you described, I am sure lesser people might have become embittered, antagonistic, and vengeful toward the object of their love – Israel – which rejected your bid for citizenship. Yet you, in a way that proves your sincerity and pure motivation, used that very experience of disappointment and rejection to shape a ministry and transform your love in a new, more mature form – one that blesses Israel and enriches Christians and Jews alike.

I echo the remarks in one Summary of your book, "The incredible life pilgrimage of Jim and Patty Hutchens gives witness to God's grace to heal, restore and re-commission to His service with renewed zeal." Indeed!

But it also gives witness to man's ability to respond to God's healing and restoration. And in the case of the Hutchens, it is a response of obedience, humility, mission and love.

Sincerely,

Rabbi Yechiel Eckstein

YE:jw

"What a wonderful, inspiring story of Jim and Patty's spiritual journey of passionate love for Jesus and sincere, compassionate love for Israel. **Guilty! is an essential book for every Christian and Jew to read.** This book builds bridges of understanding and friendship between family members of faith!"

Rev. Dr. and Mrs. Larry Keefauver
Senior Advisory Editor, *Ministries Today*

Endorsements

"Jim and Patty Hutchens' journey of faith calls us to look deep inside ourselves as Christians and ask, 'Am I willing to respond unconditionally to the call of God, whatever the price?' Their lives represent the truth and the mystery of the Jewish roots of our faith, and the Christian's living responsibility to love Israel and the Jewish people, and to seek their eternal good."

Rev. Robert Sterns
Founder, *Eagles' Wings Ministries*

"Jim Hutchens and his wife are so passionate about Israel they wanted to become Israelis. Denied citizenship, they took their case all the way to the Israeli Supreme Court. Denied again, they shook off their disappointment and found new ways to befriend the Jewish people. They've devoted their lives to encouraging Christians to stand with Israel through war and terror. Theirs is a fascinating story of one family's unconditional love for God and His people."

Joel C. Rosenberg
New York Times bestselling author of *The Last Jihad* And *The Last Days* and former senior aide to Benjamin Netanyahu and Natan Sharansky

Endorsements

"I will establish my covenant as an **everlasting covenant** between me and you and your descendants after you for the generations to come, to be your God and the God of your descendants after you. The whole land of Canaan, where you are now an alien, I will give as an **everlasting possession** to you and your descendants after you; and I will be their God."   **Genesis 17:7-8**

"Dr. Jim and Pat embarked upon a spiritual journey Prompted by their love of Israel, of the God of Israel and His Covenant. Their pilgrimage to Jerusalem and to the people of Israel engendered their desire for the heart of the Jewish faith. This book is a journey of their efforts to join their lives with God's design for His people. Jim and Pat tell a powerful story of faith and hope in their pilgrimage – a journey in search of the Holy One – a quest to be in union with God's design and purposes."

Rabbi Dr. Gerald Meister
Brooklyn, New York

Endorsements

"Guilty! is a wonderful book, the story of a remarkable couple who love each other, love Jesus and love Israel. Readers will treasure this little volume for its wisdom, historical insights and humor. One of the most interesting and informative books we've read."

Senator Bill and Ellen Armstrong
Colorado

Those Vietnam days are as real for us today as they were
then. For the men and women who went and bore the pain
and suffering of war, we owe a great debt of gratitude.
While many people back at home rioted and fought louder
and meaner about our troops being there, and while some
politicians either knowingly lied or mislead the nation, and
while a few famous Hollywood types made fools of themselves, nearly 60,000 people gave their lives for us.

... with love

My husband was nearly one of them. I argue and disagree
with Jim on many things, but every time I look at his face,
I see a brave soldier who was willing to serve his country
without whining. I see a man whom I respect and honor.
And I often quote to him from the Bible words that God
spoke to Israel, 'Oh Ephraim, Ephraim, though I often
speak against you, still I remember you, I have great
compassion for you and my heart yearns for you.'
"General Jim, my man, I'm proud of you. I salute you!"

Pat Hutchens

Contents

INTRODUCTION
The Trial

*C**an a Jew believe in Jesus and remain a Jew?* That was
the question before the Supreme Court of the State of
Israel in 1975. The High Court was about to render a land-
mark decision.

It was a decision that had been brewing since 1974
when, as a family, we applied for citizenship in the State of
Israel under the *Law of Return*, which grants automatic citizenship to any Jew who immigrates to Israel. Jews living
outside of Israel, in the "Diaspora," are considered "Exiles"
who have a right to return to the land that was their national,
ancestral homeland decreed by God's covenant.

Though we were not Jews by birth, we had undergone a
ceremonial and ritual conversion as proselytes to Judaism,
while maintaining our belief in Jesus as the Messiah. I like
to say, "When Messiah comes, he will be the same Jesus that
was born in Bethlehem."

Needless to say, our conversion was as controversial
then and it is now. Nonetheless, it was on this basis that we
had applied for citizenship in the State of Israel under the
Law of Return. During the application process, however, it
became known to the Ministry of Interior that we were, in
fact, believers in Jesus.

Consequently, the Ministry of Interior rejected our application and denied that we were qualified for citizenship

under the *Law of Return*. The reason given was that we were not Jews according to the definition of "Who is a Jew?" The definition at that time was, "A Jew is anyone who is born of a Jewish mother or has converted to Judaism." It has since been narrowed to say, "A Jew is anyone with a Jewish parent, or has converted to Judaism and does not belong to another religion."

Believing in Jesus automatically disqualified us – we were not real converts to Judaism.

At that time, when this question of Jewish identity came up, it was referred directly to the Supreme Count sitting as the High Court of Justice. And that was where our case was sent. Now we had been called to the Court to hear their decision.

The Verdict

The court room was packed. As we waited, some sat silently, some talked quietly and some had their heads bowed in prayer. The Hutchens' hearts were definitely racing and there was a tension in the air. Our case had received considerable media coverage, both in Israel and in the United States. Although most press coverage was negative, there were some brave reporters who had the courage to present views that questioned the status quo. "Why couldn't a Jew believe what he wanted to believe?" In other words, "Is there freedom of religion in Israel or not?"

In some papers, especially those speaking for the establishment, we were portrayed as wolves in sheep's clothing; as those who underhandedly wanted to change the system. One paper accused us of trying to destroy the nation and another paper depicted us as Nazis in clerical collars. It was grim. What made it even more discouraging was the fact that some of our Christian friends no longer wanted to be associated with us. One missionary who came by with good intentions said she had parked a couple of streets over and walked in the back way.

Yet, there were some stout and sturdy souls who actually wanted to be with us in that courtroom. Several were from the art community of which my wife, Patty (or Yael as she was known in Israel) was so much a part. One of these good friends was an artist who told Patty, "I know Jesus has to be the Messiah. He just has to be." When she asked how he knew, he said, "Because they keep telling us all the time he isn't." This so reminded us of a young Soviet woman who lectured in the Washington, D.C. area before the Soviet Union dismantled. She said that most of the people her age were Christians. When Pat asked how it happened, she said that the Communists had told them so many times, "There is no God," that they finally realized there had to be a God or they would not be telling everyone all of the time that there wasn't one.

One well-known Israeli artist, who had never indicated any leaning toward religious things, came on his motor cycle from Tel Aviv to be supportive. Another was a Socialist-Activist artist that Patty had exhibited with, who, though not necessarily personally religious in any way, was just appalled that any person's religious beliefs could land them in court. Yankele, an Israeli filmmaker and several people who worked on the set were there. A Four-Square-Gospel young man whose father and grandfather had been in Israel before 1948 and who had his Bible shop stoned or burned several times by the ultra-orthodox was there. A well-known Baptist Israeli scholar who had his leg blown off rescuing an Arab boy during one of Israel's wars was very supportive. Some were committed followers of Jesus, some not, some born Jews, some not, but their presence let us know that we were not alone.

One of our friends, a young man whose orthodox, Sephardic wedding we had just celebrated, said, "Yakov, (my Hebrew name in Israel), I want you to know that whatever the outcome of the trial, I consider it an honor to be here. Jesus is on trial here and this is the place I want to be. If they condemn you, I want to stand up with you."

Indeed, it was my desire that Jesus be the issue, and not the Hutchens. In this case, however, it was hard to separate the two. As I sat and pondered our fate, I realized that the situation had not really changed all that much in 2,000 years. Now, as then, when tens of thousands became his followers, everyday Israelis showed an interest in Jesus. Many others just wanted everyone to have freedom to believe as they wanted. Now, as then, it was some of the religious authorities and the political leaders who needed their support who would determine the ultimate acceptance or rejection of Jesus and his followers. Would the results be similar or would this be an opportunity for a new start? Would the establishment in Israel ever be able to accept the fact that Jesus was one of their own?

We personally knew scores of Israelis who openly said they believed Jesus to be the Messiah, and many others who believed secretly but were afraid to let it be known. Would the day ever come when Jews who believed in Jesus could be counted as a part of the modern State of Israel? We were about to find out.

We rose as the three judges who rendered the findings entered the courtroom. Once seated, each took their turn, speaking in Hebrew, making their remarks. It was not short and sweet. It was long and with increasing virulence and was a complete and total denunciation. "A Jew can be an atheist and still be a Jew. A Jew can be a Buddhist and still be a Jew. But never, under any circumstances, can a Jew ever believe in Jesus and still be a Jew." One judge wrote, "There is that sect of Jews who turn into believers in Jesus, but Israel vomits them out. They will have no place in the House of Israel." And on and on it went.

We were stunned and numbed.

We were devastated.

CHAPTER 1

Leaving Israel

Within a week we received a letter from the Ministry of the Interior which read in part, "You have thirty days to finalize your affairs and leave Israel. If you do not comply you will be subject to fine, imprisonment or both." That was it – it was over.

But how could it be over? Were we not called to this? Was this not God's plan for us?

Rejection always has some collateral damage, like shame and embarrassment. It is both humbling and humiliating. Did we really deserve this? Why? Why? Why? Had we not come to Israel to make our home and to raise our family? We even fully expected that our children would serve in the Israeli Army when their time came. Had we totally missed God's calling and direction? What had gone wrong? Was it that my sins were so deep that God can't use me? Does he only use those sinless and perfect? Although I knew that wasn't right, biblically, those questions still arose. But what was right? Not only were we swirling in a sea of rejection but it fast became a sea of confusion. To find oneself totally rejected with no plans for the future was a hard place indeed.

Like it or not, that was the state we were in. Now we had to pack up quickly and leave the country. First, that meant getting the children ready emotionally to leave their friends and schoolmates. For the past two years they had been in Israeli public schools. They were well into Israeli culture and were very much at home with the Hebrew language. Our daughters, Sarah and Rachel, spoke Hebrew like Israelis, as did our son Matt, who had excelled in school, had been chosen to go to a special engineering high school in Tel Aviv - and had gone through a Bar Mitzvah. This was going to be a monumental change for our whole family – one with bittersweet memories.

One of those memories is of the day Patty and the children left to return to the States. Our flight from Lod airport (now Ben Gurion International Airport) was scheduled to leave at 7:30 AM. That meant we had to be up and ready to go three hours before. As we walked out the door at about 4:30 AM, none of us will ever forget what and who greeted us. The whole front yard was filled with Israeli kids who were classmates of our children. Many of these kids had spent the night in sleeping bags in the front yard. Many of their parents were there as well. Everyone knew all the particulars of our recent trial and the decision that had come down, and they came as a show of friendship and support.

There were tears and hugs, gifts and flowers. The head of the school where the children had been for two years came and in a gracious, loving gesture, refunded the money we had paid for the last two years of school fees. One neighbor came with a baseball bat and said he just hoped one of the ultra orthodox would show up to harass us. The man who owned the small grocery store at the end of the street, where everyone shopped and charged food, came and told us to forget about paying our bill until we were back in America and settled. These good friends made our leaving a little easier, giving us a safe cushion for the future recovery from the blows which we had received.

The Volvo

I had to stay in Israel in order to sell our only valuable possession. It was a 1975 Volvo station wagon that had been given to us brand new. It was well worth $6,000.00, which I figured would cover the $4,000.00 airfare to get us all home, plus a little to live on until we got established back in the USA. I put several ads in newspapers and had several inquiries, however there were no offers. The fifteen days were running out and I needed to sell this car. One Friday evening I went to some friends' home for Shabbat dinner. During the course of the evening I was told by this couple that they were praying for a new vehicle for the transportation needs of their music ministry. I thought perhaps they might be interested and told them about the station wagon and they agreed that it would be the perfect car. There was only one problem—they didn't have enough money to buy a good car. We left it at that and had a good dinner; then I went home.

That night I did not sleep a wink. I kept getting this strong impression that I should give our car to this couple. I could not believe that this was an impression from God. Didn't He know it would leave us flat broke with absolutely no visible means of support. I tossed and turned all night, fighting this crazy notion that I was supposed to give away this car. Finally, I told the Lord, "This is your car; you can do with it what you want."

I seemed to get an even stronger impression in my spirit that He was saying, "Good. If this is really my car, then I want you to give away." I could not believe I was hearing this.

All the next day I wrestled with the implications of giving the car away. "Patty is going to be devastated," I thought. "She left the country only because she trusted me to sell this car and come home to provide for the family. We will have absolutely nothing to live on. How will I pay for the airline tickets which I charged on my credit card? It is simply not good sense and God would require that of me, especially after having been kicked out of the country where we felt sure God had called us to serve." These thoughts swirled in my mind. Was I right? Or, wrong? There was no peace that day and I slept little or none Saturday night either.

Early Sunday morning I finally gave in. "All right," I told the Lord, "if you want me to give this car away, I'll do it, but I need some kind of confirmation from your Word." Almost immediately I was lead to Mark 10:29-31:

> *Jesus said, "Truly, I say to you, there is no one who has left house or brothers or sisters or mother or father or children or lands, for my sake and for the gospel, who will not receive a hundredfold now in this time, houses and brothers and sisters and mothers and children and lands, with persecutions, and in the age to come eternal life. But many who are first will be last, and the last first."*

I began to sense that this was what I had to do. Still, I would need God's grace to actually do this. I called my friend on the phone and said, "Sit down. You need to know that what I am about to tell you is definitely of the Lord. It is certainly not of me, because if I had my way about it I wouldn't be doing it. As a matter of fact, I can't believe I am going to do this, but I don't have my way about it. So here it is. I believe God wants me to give you our car."

There was silence on the other end. Then, "It's a good thing you told me to sit down, otherwise I probably would have fainted dead away. Jim, I know this is very difficult for you but I also want you to know how deeply grateful we are."

"You need to be grateful to the Lord," I told him,

"because He is the one who is providing it, not me." He understood, and from the reports we heard over the years, that ministry was greatly blessed by God. I was glad to have some small part in spite my reluctance.

But now I had face Patty. I called her on the telephone, "Hi Honey, everything is taken care of with the car, I'll be home on the next plane."

"Did you sell it?" she asked.

"Everything is taken care of," I assured her. There was an absolute lull.

"You gave it away, didn't you?" Now I was silent, trying to think of what I could say, when she pressed, "You gave that car away, didn't you, Jim Hutchens? I know you did – you gave it away – you just gave it away, didn't you?" She even said the names of the couple to whom I had given the car.

Meekly I told her, "Yes, I did. I had to. I didn't really want to give it away, but the Lord woke me up in the middle of the night and I heard in my spirit, 'Give them the car.'" Now there was real silence on the American side of the ocean.

"I had to do it, Patty, I had to do it. Remember God promises a hundredfold blessing when we give." Patty was crying now and quietly said, "We'll talk when you get home, Jim." Then she hung up the phone.

Now with the family back in the States and the car was gone, I had nothing to do but wait for the plane and think about what had happened. The verdict was in. We had been found guilty by the Supreme Court of the State of Israel. Guilty of what? Guilty of attempting to immigrate under the *Law of Return*, as Jews who believed in Jesus.

We failed in efforts to try to identify with the Jewish people and immigrate under the *Law of Return*. The desires of our hearts had been dashed. We were rejected by a nation we loved and believed in, a nation with a special place in the plan of God that we wanted to share. Did we totally misunderstand the leading and guidance of God?

And to add insult to injury, we were broke. We had spent all our savings, all our retirements funds, had cashed in insurance policies to make the move and now we had scarcely a dime to our name. We had charged the airline tickets back to the States for the family and all our belongings and we would soon have to pay. The future looked dark and foreboding.

Feeling broken and humiliated, I asked myself, "How on earth did we get here? How could it have come to this?" What kind of father and husband would give up security and paying jobs to take his wife and family through such ordeals? Our hopes and aspirations had seemed so noble, so grounded in the God's Holy Scriptures. What had gone wrong?

I needed some answers. Perhaps the place to begin was to retrace our steps from the beginning — but first, I want you to hear from Patty.

Patty's Perspective

Even to this day I can recall almost blow by blow our going before the Supreme Court of Israel. My brother Max Mercer, a prominent and very successful lawyer in New Orleans, Louisiana, had helped me in the past with legal matters and had promised to be there early in the morning on the date set for the trial. As we finished dressing and were having breakfast before driving to Jerusalem, a knock came at the door. I was so sure it was Max. I ran to the door but was handed a telegram from my brother, saying, "Sorry, I can't be there. Stop. Jewish friends here in New Orleans say it wouldn't help anyway. Stop. Love, Max. Stop."

I knew one of those friends was a Jewish federal judge in Louisiana. He had purchased one of my etchings when a few months earlier I had an art exhibition at Studio 8 in New Orleans. Tears rolled down my face knowing that my big brother would not be there beside me. After that, I should have known things would not turn out well. In fact, although I did not find it out until a few days later, that very day Max had a car wreck that crushed his heart and ripped into one of his lungs. When I heard it, I knew he must have felt angry, guilty or both - perhaps he wasn't his usual, alert self and had a wreck.

I was told he was hurt so badly that although he pleaded in the hospital for someone to pray for him, the doctors and nurses could only keep working fast and feverishly, saying nothing. Finally a black attendant came over and said, "Mr. Mercer, I will pray for you." I have never met that man but I often think of him, hoping one day I will know his name.

Max was able to survive but his health was severely affected and he suffered from extreme asthma and poor health the rest of his life. He later died from an asthma attack while in the hospital at Slidell, Louisiana. He was only 46 years old. I have always considered Max as one of the casualties most wounded by our Israel experience.

Now I had to face this trial with no lawyer brother. Abandonment is the word that still comes to mind. However, we had our children to think of, so we tried to compose ourselves and go on, praying as we drove the long road up to Jerusalem. When we got to the courtroom, one of the guards pointed to Rachel, our smallest child and said, "She can't go in. The older two can sit with you but she is too young. She will have to go with me and a woman will stay with her."

Rachel looked at me as her eyes grew larger, but I bowed down and whispered in her ear, "You are not going anywhere, baby, just start crying." And she did. I mean she was *really* crying, so much so that it got the attention of the judges. After the guard went to speak with them, one of the judges announced, "She can stay." Then we began. For the rest, I simply want to quote a long letter I wrote a day or two after the trial.

Long Letter of Reflection

"We went to the Supreme Court to receive the answer to our trial. To this day, it stills seems crazy to me — the word *trial*. My family was always on the side of law and order, with lawyers, teachers, congressmen, senators, and we always had pounded into us that we must respect the law, that a man is innocent till proven guilty, that no country could stand without proper constitutions and laws.

"To have found ourselves even *on* the 'condemned' side in a court room was bad enough – but to get the response we did was truly shocking. On that morning when we got to the courtroom, we were informed that our lawyer would not be there, only his assistant. That was not a good sign. Right away, I felt it had to be bad.

"The courtroom was crowded with new trials for the morning, and decisions were simply read in brief. Ours was second, and the judge read so quietly that I hardly heard what was said, only that the order to the Ministry of Interior (to show cause why we should not be registered) was cancelled and we were fined 5,000 pounds. The assistant then signaled to us and we went outside. He said that we had lost, that sometimes appeals were made, but in our case he would not suggest it. We had the transcript sent down to us the next day and after getting someone to translate it, we really saw the weight of what was said.

"The next morning in the newspapers, we were accused of 'a criminal plot to destroy the faith of the Jewish people,' among other things. This 'plot' was carried out according to the judges, by 'donations of members of this community of the Brethren sect.'

"One judge said that we asked friends to "keep things in secret from the evil eye" (he was making a reference to Jews). The legal affidavit, which a reputable Jewish lawyer of Chicago made when he and I went to see the Rabbi who converted us, was totally dismissed by the Court. They said it was not possible for an orthodox Rabbi to say such things.

"In the affidavit, the lawyer swore on pain of perjury that the Rabbi had admitted that he did know of our beliefs in Jesus, but that his 'hands were tied.' He said that a Rabbi Dolgin from Israel had personally come to Chicago and threatened him, saying if he did not cancel our conversion, all conversions from the Chicago Rabbinical Council would be treated just like Conservative and Reform conversions – 'not worth the paper they are written on.'

"This affidavit was dismissed because the judge said, 'It appears extremely peculiar in the mouth of an orthodox Jewish rabbi,' and was 'inconceivable' to them.' The judge went on to *imagine* a situation, then said it could not be so, therefore he said it wasn't so. Naturally, with this affidavit out of the way and with the refusal to see the obvious lack of due process, we were accused of 'fraud,' and the judges said that we had remained 'Jesuit Christians.' I recall thinking, I wish we were Jesuits; we might get some real help.

"The summation of it all I (the judge speaking) quote here, '**About Jesus persons who are considered to be and accepted as Jews we have not yet heard. The thing is simply not reasonable. According to any standard, be it halachic-religious or legal-secular, there is no such thing. Ask, if you will, a Jew in the street if such a thing is possible, and his certain answer will be 'No.' It is known that there is a sect of people who were *born Jews* and turned into believers in Jesus the messiah, which are called 'Hebrew-Christian.' They apparently want to keep their Jewish origin, but Judaism vomited them out from within, and they shall not be in the congregation of Israel.'**

"This was May 19, 1976. Some of the papers even said that if Judaism had vomited out natural-born Jews who believed in Jesus, how much more so converts.

"Not only had we been vomited out, but as I walked out

of the courtroom that day in Jerusalem, the same Rabbi Dolgin that the Chicago rabbi had referred too, looked me right in the eyes and called me "Zonah," a Hebrew word meaning "whore." I held myself together long enough to pass by the judges bench and then exited the courtroom doing what I did a lot of in those days, I sobbed.

"Well, frankly, I went to bed for a few days. The isolation of that first week afterwards was, to say the least, traumatic. I am still unable to really see the entire situation in a proper perspective. Our immediate problem was the 5,000 pounds and God moved on the hearts of several people in Israel, both Jews and Christians, and they collected the entire amount almost immediately. We also still owed about four thousand dollars and we owed the lawyer in Chicago eight hundred dollars. Jim wrote checks for about $4,000.00 in one day, and our bank account was left with a sum total of $71. We like to call that faith. We got a call last night from one Jewish believer who was sending a check today for $2500. And we are so thankful.

"The reactions have been varied. Some of our friends have simply dropped off (both Christians and Jews). A few courageous ones have come by to express deep regrets. Several artist friends have especially been encouraging. One called and said, "Yael, my dear, I have called to give aid and comfort." Jim has spent a great deal of time in deep soul searching and prayer, trying to see the meaning in it all, and to hear from God what our next steps are. Pray for him as he leads the family in these decisions.

"A family of 37 Messianic Jews were given notice today by the Prime Minister's office that they would have to leave their farming community in the area of Eilat. Most feel there is nothing that can be done in light of the heavy-handed response, and several newspapers who were formerly interested said now they are not. One man did come interview us and wrote a somewhat positive article. We were told by one politician he was probably the only Israeli who had the nerve to write it. We were given only a month extension on our visa by the Ministry of Interior.

"It is difficult to know really what to do. We know that Messianic Judaism is not understood and since it really is a new movement, except for in the beginning when it was *the norm* for Jewish believers, it will have its growing pains. But this prejudiced response by the chief justices of the Land of Israel referring to people as being 'vomited out' is difficult to access. Do pray for this man, Judge Berenson.

"One thing that gave me great comfort – on the very day that our case was reported in the newspapers as a 'plot,' there was an extended article about the movie, 'Passover Plot,' which is being filmed here. Of course in this film (which is taken from the book of the same name) Jesus is accused of making a plot, faking death, and setting himself up as the Messiah. It was some comfort to see the same word used.

"There has been much controversy over this film being done here, and the government has given the standard money given to encourage making films here in Israel, though saying there is no 'official' connection. If such a film were made in Israel about Muhammed, there would no doubt be a 'holy war.' We are praying that this film will be stopped as it will only bring harm to Israel.

"It seems that when difficulties come, they come all at the same time. The very day after we received our 'judgment' my brother Max was to call us. Instead, when the call came, it was my sister, Wam, and she said that Max was almost killed in a car wreck. A large truck filled with sand hit him on the driver's side. He had a concussion, deep gashes on his face that required plastic surgery, broken arms, broken ribs, pierced lungs, a hole in one side and a mashed and bruised heart.

"My first response was despair, but then I felt I had to get myself together to pray for him. How grateful to God we are that an ambulance was right there near, and after several hours of surgery in a fine hospital in New Orleans he is going to recover. Do pray for him and for his wife and children.

"A definite turning point came in my life here one day after all this happened. My 77- year-old mother called. Many of you have heard about her before, of her tried but unshakable faith, and that with a lifetime of trials. When she called, I was instantly encouraged just to hear her voice. I said, 'Mama, they called us 'criminals' in the papers.'

She said, 'Honey, you know it doesn't matter what people call you. We are concerned only with Truth.'

I said, 'We may get sent back.' Without even a change in tone, she said 'Well, let's see, I have twin beds in one room, a double in the extra bedroom and a hide-a-bed. Don't worry, baby, we have plenty of room.'

'But Mama,' I pleaded as I began to weep, 'It's hard!'

She immediately responded, 'Honey, we never said it wouldn't be hard. Life is hard. It's hard everywhere!'

Finally I asked, 'Do you have any special words of encouragement for me?' and my good mother answered, 'Just remember that Jesus said, I'll never leave you or forsake you. That's all you have to remember.' Then we talked a little longer and after I hung up I said, 'Thank God for a mother like that.'

"We are beginning to come out of the situation enough to at least see. The children have taken it well, and are going on as usual in the Israeli schools. Matt has built himself a little house in the back yard, with a foundation, windows, etc. He builds fires at night and reads. One night we heard wonderful strains of Bach on the radio he has out there. He and his Israeli friends (from Ramat HaSharon) were sitting around on sawed-off logs in the little room, listening to classical music.

"We have tried to continue life as normal in an abnormal

world. I am planning an art exhibit of Western portraits on the 21st of June – perhaps the last exhibit I'll have here. We need your prayers. Fight for your faith and for your freedom and for the right to believe and live your beliefs."

And so ends the long letter, and the recalling of how we were found, **Guilty**!

Now let us tell you how it all started.

CHAPTER 2

In the Beginning

The journey of faith recorded in this book reveals a pilgrimage, yes, even a call, that Patty and I have shared for much of our married life. At times, we have faltered. Sometimes we have gone on in the midst of rejection and failure and sometimes there was fear. But we always knew that by God's grace we could continue.

Sometimes a call becomes so faint you can barely hear it. At times, the noise of competing causes can all but drown out a call. Following a call can be difficult, even torturous at times, but a call on one's life remains, *"For the gifts and the calling of God are irrevocable"* (Romans 11:29). For me, the seeds of the call were sown early in my life as a Christian.

Soldiering

1956 was a good year—a very good year. In January 1956, I came to faith in Jesus Christ as my Lord and Redeemer. I was stationed at Fort Campbell, Kentucky, serving as an enlisted man with the 511th Airborne Infantry Regiment of the 11th Airborne Division. I had just joined the unit in September of 1955, after finishing Basic Training at Fort Leonard Wood, Missouri. Like all newly assigned men to the unit, I had a brief interview with our regimental chaplain, First Lieutenant Burt Hatch.

First impressions of Chaplain Hatch were very positive.

He was a man's man and very likable. He was the first clergyman with whom I'd ever had an extended conversation. While I had grown up in a nominally Christian home, looking back I realize it was just assumed everybody was a Christian. Time proved that was not a correct assumption. Like many little boys, my single-mom mother took me to a local church, probably hoping it would influence me to stay out of trouble. I do remember hearing some of the stories from the Old Testament.

However, if the good news of Jesus as Savior from the penalty of sin was preached, either I wasn't ready for it or it went right past me. Maybe some of both. I wasn't really hostile toward religion; it just didn't relate to me.

By the time I was approaching teenage years, church was a thing of the past for my buddies and me. Most of those years were spent acting like many teenagers who do not have a father at home and who make up their own rules. Those years were lonely, dark and morally dismal, years filled with aimlessness, emptiness and lack of purpose.

In fact, in a way I was trying my best to go to hell as fast as I could. And I nearly made it - several times. I knew I needed help, but I didn't have the slightest idea where to go to get it. Eventually, I volunteered for the draft in the Army just to get out of town and try to find some answers - any answers.

My first extended meeting with Chaplain Hatch came about because a friend of mine who wanted to get out of the Army had an appointment with him. He wanted to see if the Chaplain could help him get a Hardship Discharge because of family problems. My friend was afraid even to go into a chapel alone and asked me to go with him. While he was talking with another chaplain in his office and I was waiting in the narthex, Chaplain Hatch came out of his office and greeted me.

There I was talking again with Chaplain Hatch, a man so

completely different from my conception of a clergyman. I realize now it was a providential appointment, but this initial interview with the Chaplain was just a nice, low-key, friendly talk. In an effort to add something meaningful to the conversation, I told him I had questions about things I had heard and read in the Bible. I'm sure he sensed I didn't know anything about the Bible but he was gracious and suggested I write down my questions so we could get together later and talk about them. So, I did.

During the fall of 1955, I probably made ten visits to his office and we discussed my questions. Each visit got more interesting. He had given me a Bible that first day and I began to thumb through and search for something I recognized. I first found the story of Jonah. Why didn't Jonah die in the belly in the whale? There was a good question. Or who was Cain's wife? Or could Judas be forgiven? Amazingly, when I presented each question to the Chaplain he took me right back to the Bible for an answer that always seemed reasonable and satisfying.

However, in January of 1956, at Chapel 11 on Indiana Avenue at Fort Campbell, Kentucky, Chaplain Hatch had a question for me. He said, "Jim, we've been talking about spiritual matters now for some time. We've talked about what Christ has done on the cross, as our substitute, to pay the penalty for our sins and what the Bible has to say about your questions."

He continued, "Let me ask you this. Have you ever placed your faith in Jesus Christ as your own personal Savior?" I was a little taken back at first, but then I asked, "What do you mean by faith?" His answer was a life-changing event.

He said, "Let me explain it this way." Then he took a quarter from his pocket and held it out in front of me and said, "I'm going to give you this quarter. Do you believe me?"

"Yes Sir," I said, "I believe you."

"But how can you be sure?" he asked.

37

"Well, I trust you. You are a man of the cloth. I believe you will do what you say."

He pressed on, "But how can you be absolutely sure I'll give this quarter?"

I was beginning to get it and cautiously answered, "If I reach out and take it?"

"Then do it!" As I reached out to take the quarter, at the same time he reached out and took hold of my hand. "Jim, that is the hand of faith," he told me, "and you could sit there and believe and believe indefinitely, but until you reach out in faith and receive the quarter I'm offering you, it will never be yours, right?" That made sense to me.

He went on, "The same thing is true of the gift that God has given us in Jesus Christ. If we don't reach out in faith and receive it, we don't get it. If we don't invite him to come into our lives to be our Savior, to forgive us our sins, to be Lord of our lives, he doesn't come in. Does that make sense?" Of course it did. "If it does," he suggested, "then why don't we finalize that decision right now? Why don't we pray? Could we do that?"

"Sure," I said.

"Then why don't I lead us in prayer and you repeat after me. Is that okay with you?"

"Sure" I said, "I can do that."

Then he prayed, "Gracious heavenly Father, I come to you in Jesus' name." I repeated after him. "I confess that I have sinned and that I am a sinner." I repeated the words. "And I ask you to forgive all my sins." I was right with him word for word.

"I ask you to fill me with your Holy Spirit. I pray that you will take complete control of my life and lead me in the way you want me to go. I give my life to you from this day forward to do with as you please. With thanksgiving, I offer this prayer in Jesus' name. Amen." Phrase by phrase I had repeated the whole prayer.

Afterward I looked up and asked, "Is that all there is to it?" He assured me, "Don't make it more difficult than it is. Receiving Jesus Christ is a decision of the will, not a result of our works. This is the beginning of something special. Welcome to the Lord's family."

As you are reading this book, if you want to take this step of faith, I invite you to pray in your own words just as I did and receive Jesus as your Lord and Savior.

Indeed, it *was* the beginning of something special, a spiritual event that one can only experience. Certainly there have been some extremely difficult times since that January day in 1956. But in the midst of those times, there has always been Someone I could turn to. Someone who understood what I was going through. Someone who stood by me.

That huge hole of meaninglessness and emptiness in my heart was amazingly filled from that day to this. I have known since that day that He will never leave me or forsake me.

It was a great way to begin 1956. But it got better. It was during that first year as a follower of Jesus Christ that the seeds were sown regarding Israel, seeds that later sprouted and grew into a call to service. It was not a single event but rather a growing process. Here's how it emerged.

The Birthing of Israel

I had an intense desire to learn more about my newfound faith. Chaplain Hatch sensed that desire and began to lend me a steady stream of books from his personal library. In addition, I learned of a group of young paratroopers who were memorizing Scripture in a program started by the Navigators. It was called "B Rations," patterned after the Army's nomenclature for dispensing food. It was exactly what I needed at the time and is something I have continued to practice throughout my life as Christian.

But most important in shaping my thinking, especially

with respect to Israel, was the Bible study led each week by Chaplain Hatch. There he taught me the significance of Israel in the mind and will of God and the special role God has for Israel leading up to the return of Christ. Even then I was intrigued with the events that had surrounded the Jewish people just in my lifetime.

The Holocaust had been, and remains, the formative event in Jewish history in the 20th century. That six million Jews had been systematically exterminated by the Third Reich, supposedly an enlightened and civilized nation, was then and is today mind-boggling. And why? Simply because they were Jews.

Out of that horrific experience, however, came the miraculous birth of State of Israel in 1948. In retrospect, it is perhaps safe to say that somehow within the deep mysteries of God's providence, had the Holocaust not taken place, probably there would have been no modern State of Israel. The dynamics of world opinion were ripened at that time to follow the lead of President Truman's immediate recognition of Israel. That decision by the United States prepared the way for the acceptance of Israel as a sovereign nation by the larger community of nations in the United Nations.

In our Bible studies with Chaplain Hatch, all contemporary and political realities were screened through the Covenant promises of God to ancient Israel, as well as the prophetic Scriptures of both the Old and New Testaments. Indeed, the seeds were sown and nurtured in those Bible studies and discussions with Chaplain Hatch which developed in me a deep love and support for Israel that later would later come to a fuller fruition.

College

Following my tour of duty as an enlisted man in the Army, I enrolled at Wheaton College in Wheaton, Illinois. Chaplain Hatch was also instrumental in making this happen.

After my application had been initially turned down because of poor high school grades, he wrote a letter to the registrar. Whatever he said must have been convincing because I soon after received a letter saying I had been accepted on probation for summer school. After finishing a successful summer school experience (in fact my first successful school experience, period), I was fully accepted for enrollment the coming year. My new life in Christ had been given a new motivation and purpose for living.

Wheaton was a grand experience. It was there a Christian worldview began to take shape, and for me there was always, gentle on my mind, the place of Israel in this worldview. The growing and stretching of a Christian liberal arts education was exhilarating. In addition, I was able to play football again, the sport that had been my favorite in high school. Those were good years for Wheaton football and I was privileged to be a starter my last two years, one an undefeated season, placing third in the nation in small colleges.

Patty!

But most important was my meeting with a very special, lovely, young lady from Louisiana, Patty Mercer. She had honey-blond hair and the most beautiful blue eyes I had ever seen. It was definitely chemistry at first sight. Love was soon to follow. I had never formed a mental profile of the perfect wife, but I had always thought it would be icing on the cake if she could play the piano, since that has always been one of my favorite forms of music. Wouldn't you know? Patty played the piano!

Although I assumed that a Christian college was an excellent place to meet a potential Christian wife, I had not counted on meeting her in September of the first year. In fact, I had determined beforehand that my priorities in college would be:

1) Academics
2) Athletics
3) Extracurricular activities, which included girls.

Meeting Patty changed my priorities!

After having several dates with Patty, she asked me to attend a weekend Young Life conference in Kenosha, Wisconsin. I knew little about this group, but she had been involved with Young Life since high school and was now on student staff. During the ride back from the conference, Patty asked me a very direct question, "Jim, what do you want to do with your life?"

I sensed she was going somewhere with this question. "I just want to finish school and serve the Lord," I told her.

She wanted more. "How specifically would you like to serve the Lord?" I had to admit I wasn't sure. Her next question was thought provoking, but also disturbing.

Patty said, "Let me ask you this. If you could do anything in the world, and were sure you wouldn't fail, what would you do?" Wow! Talk about a direct question.

After I thought a few moments, it came to me, "You know the Army has been very good to me. It's where I came to know the Lord and for the first time got a real sense of purpose for my life. I was greatly helped by an Army Chaplain. If I could, although I know I am in no way qualified for it, I would like to serve the Lord as an Army Chaplain."

"Good," she said, "Why don't you do just that? Head in that direction and we'll pray if that's what the Lord wants, He'll open the necessary doors, and if not, He'll close the doors."

That sounded right to me, but I reminded her that to follow that course, I would have to go to seminary. Patty didn't miss a beat and said, "Yes, that's the way it looks to me too. Let's do it."

I picked up immediately on the "let's" aspect and it sounded promising. The very next day I went to the library and began to check through various seminary directories.

Obviously, my relationship with Patty was on fast forward and both of us were excited about what we both felt God had for us together. On November 11, 1958 (Veterans Day, to be exact), I officially proposed to Patty and gave her an engagement ring I had been saving money for months to buy. The following June 9, 1959, we were married. Her mother had made her promise she would not marry until she finished college, so we married the day *after* she graduated.

Because of work and Army years, I still had one year left in college, so Patty taught junior high school in Bellwood, Illinois while I finished my last year to graduate in 1960. Then, it was "Seminary, here we come."

Seminary

Dallas Theological Seminary in Dallas, Texas, was the school I chose because I had been so impressed with Dallas grads whom I had met and heard during my Wheaton experience. Dr. Carl Armerding, one of my Bible teachers at Wheaton, was one of the Dallas men we heard speak many times in chapel, and his capacity for biblical exposition, preaching and teaching was legend. I thought the seminary he attended would be able to equip me for the chaplaincy and the ministry in general.

Indeed, the Dallas experience was a very positive experience, especially since two of our three children were born there. Our son Matt was born on April 6, 1962, Palm Sunday, and Sarah on January 31, 1964, the birthday of Felix Mercer, Patty's father. Our daughter Rachel was born later in 1968 while we were with the Green Berets at Ft. Devens, Massachusetts. All three are married now with wonderful Christian spouses, all live near us in Virginia, and we have a total of eleven grandchildren. Indeed, as Psalm

127 says, *"Behold, children are a heritage from the Lord. The fruit of the womb is a reward. Like arrows in the hand of a warrior, are the children of one's youth. Blessed is the man (and woman) who has his quiver full of them."* Our quiver is definitely full.

In addition to studying Hebrew and Greek for four years, I regard many of the professors at Dallas Seminary as spiritual fathers in the faith, especially with respect to my understanding of Israel in the plans and purposes of God. Those seeds sown earlier with the Army Chaplain were now being nurtured and gradually taking shape. The eternal, unconditional nature of God's covenant with Abraham, restated to Isaac and Jacob, had particular relevance to the modern State of Israel, an obvious, contemporary fulfillment of God's ancient promises.

At that time, I had little understanding of the notion of "Replacement Theology." That would come much later when I learned that from the 3rd century on, most of Christianity, including both Catholic and main-line Protestantism, has viewed Christians and the Church as having replaced or superceded (hence, Supersessionism) the Jews and Israel as the covenant people of God. Over the centuries, this tragic error has served as a spiritual imprimatur for the justification of the most grotesque forms of anti-Semitism, which had its ultimate expression in the massacre of six million Jews by the Nazi war machine. But more on that subject later.

During my seminary training I attended the U.S. Army Chaplain's School Basic Course, located at that time at Fort Slocum, just outside New York City. With our new baby Matt sleeping on a mattress in a Zee Tissues carton box, we traveled by Volkswagen from Texas to New York for the summer of 1962. As only God could have arranged it, Chaplain Burt Hatch and his family were stationed at Fort Slocum and he was on the faculty of the Chaplain's School.

He and his dear wife Marie graciously invited Patty and baby Matt to stay with them that summer while I was in school. What a gift!

That summer prepared me for going on active duty after graduating from seminary in the spring of 1964. That is exactly what happened after I received orders in May to report to Fort Campbell, Kentucky on July 1, 1964. To top it all off, I was assigned to Chapel 11 on Indiana Avenue, the very place I had received Christ eight years before under the ministry of Chaplain Hatch. Isn't God amazing!

Back to the Army—Vietnam

Indeed, this was like coming home. But now I had my family with me. Patty loved the military, having had a father and two brothers in the Navy. (I never held it against them.) However, soon the rumor mill began to circulate that Vietnam was probably going to be in the future for most of us at Fort Campbell, the home of the 101st Airborne Division.

I became increasingly aware that this was a very real possibility and sensing the reality of that future, I wanted to be as prepared as possible.

With that in mind, I volunteered for the U.S. Army's Ranger School and in January of 1965 attended the school for nine weeks of the most grueling physical and emotional training I have ever undergone. But it was well worth it and did serve to prepare me as much as anything could for what was coming—Vietnam.

The order finally came down and we were scheduled to leave August 1, 1965. We had already decided that for the year I was gone, Patty and the children would go back to Wheaton, where she had a part-time teaching position in the Art Department. It was a quiet, but emotional and solemn parting at Fort Campbell. We walked the kids over to a baseball game being played near the Transient Officer Quarters where we were staying. We had a light dinner together, got the kids down with a special time of prayer, and then spent a long time just looking at each other. There were no tears then. It was just good to be together, and we both hoped and prayed it would not be for the last time.

From a service and ministry standpoint, Vietnam was very rewarding. Although it's tough being separated from one's family with the daily awareness it might be for good, there was great satisfaction in serving the soldiers in real spiritual ways. I had the Protestant, Catholic and Jewish prayer books to draw on for dying soldiers, and as is usually the case in wartime, many men and women (mostly nurses at that time) came to faith in Jesus Christ that year. Many grew in their knowledge of the Lord and developed a more mature walk with Him. Being in combat definitely brings almost everyone to the awareness of the need for God—for Someone to care and watch over them.

Soldiers ask basic questions when faced with the prospect of for-real combat and death. *Why am I here? What is my purpose in life? Is there life after death? Is there a God and if so, how can I know Him?*

For a chaplain, that is an environment ripe for real service and ministry. Indeed, we sensed God's blessing and watch-care in many special ways during that year in Vietnam.

Hill 65

That was particularly true during my closest encounter with what many people called "the Grim Reaper." On November 8, 1965, I was serving with the 1st Battalion (Airborne) 503rd Infantry of the 173d Airborne Brigade. We were on *Operation Hump.* We had gone out at dawn on a platoon-size patrol with Charlie Company under the command of Captain Henry Tucker. He was rightly called "Big Tuck," for he was six foot six and had played defensive end at "Ole Miss." After about an hour we found ourselves smack in the middle of an all-out firefight. We had been ambushed.

We backed off and formed a perimeter, much like circling the wagons in a western movie, and the fight was on. About 11 a.m. when the firing subsided somewhat, we could hear the cries of one of our men out front who had been hit at the start of the ambush. We determined that it was our point man and he was being used as bait by the Viet Cong to get us to come out and rescue him.

This was a proven tactic of the VC. They would shoot-to-wound a point man, knowing that the Americans never leave their dead or wounded behind. Then when a rescue team came out to get the wounded man, they would fire on the rescuers, killing or wounding as many of them as possible. It was a vicious tactic, but it worked. Certainly, it was our plan to get the wounded man, but we had to wait for a lull in the heavy firing.

Sensing that lull, Charlie Company's First Sergeant, Master Sergeant Edgar Board, came to me and two others and said, "Now's the time, we need to go out and get him." With that the three of us began to move cautiously toward the sound of the soldier's cries. Once we found him, we put him on a makeshift litter (actually an Army blanket), and each one grabbed a corner and began to carry him back toward the inside of the perimeter.

Then it happened. As we knew they would, the VC opened fire on us. One of our men was killed instantly and the other two of us were wounded. I was hit across the chest and stomach and a round lodged in my upper thigh. I was able, however, to get my arm around one of the other soldiers who had been hit in the back and couldn't walk, and drag him back to safety. Later another rescue team went back out and got the wounded soldier we had initially gone out to rescue, plus a dead soldier still there.

Joel

That was the battle of Hill 65. Up until that point in the Vietnam, Hill 65 was the largest and most intense battle of the war. Through it all, there was one man whose heroics stand out in bold relief for me—our medic, Specialist Lawrence Joel. Sp.5 Joel was a quiet, unassuming, but very professional medic. He was the kind of medic you would want with you in a firefight. Early in the fight, however, Joel had been wounded. Yet, for the next 24 hours while the battle raged, Joel continued to move forward, often unarmed, to carry back the wounded.

Although he received multiple wounds during that time, it was as though there was a shield of protection about him. Joel was indeed, the "Wounded Healer." It seemed as though God said to the destroyer, "You can go this far and no farther with my servant Joel."

After I had been hit, Joel treated me as best he could under the circumstances and I had to remain at the aid station with a badly bleeding and progressively stiffening leg, making it very difficult to move. I was able to get around to the wounded Joel was bringing back to the aid station and offer a prayer here, a word of Scripture there or sometimes just hold the tightly grasping hand of a dying soldier and pray for him. Through the night, what I observed in Joel was a miracle in the making. He was fearless and seemed indestructible. God fashioned a genuine hero before our eyes and he was truly something to behold.

After we returned to our base camp at Ben Hoa, several of us shared our observations of Joel's exploits. We all agreed that this man must be cited for heroism above and beyond the call of duty. We each wrote up our corroborating accounts and recommended he be considered for the Distinguished Service Cross, the second highest combat award given in the U.S. Army.

When our battalion commander, Lieutenant Colonel John

Tyler read the citation and the corroborating accounts, he immediately upgraded the recommendation to the Congressional Medal of Honor. One year later, Sp.6 Lawrence Joel, the first black medic in Vietnam, was awarded the Congressional Medal of Honor by President Lyndon Johnson. No CMH recipient was ever more deserving.

Joel stayed on in the Army and retired as a Sergeant First Class. I had lost contact with him, but in 1984 received a call from his family. Joel had died and they asked if I would conduct his funeral at Arlington National Cemetery at Fort Myer, Virginia. It was very sad to hear of Joel's passing, but I felt a deep honor in being able to officiate at the funeral of this great American hero. I wrote of that day of Joel's exploits in my book, *"Beyond Combat."*

The war was brought back to me with a sobering reality the day I conducted Joel's funeral at the Post Chapel at Fort Myer, Virginia, on February 13, 1984. As I looked out on the chapel, there at the funeral were many of the men who had been together that day on Hill 65. The Secretary of the Army, John Marsh, paid his respects. The chapel was packed. Commanders and soldiers sat side by side.

Silently everyone sat and listened to the doleful sounds of the Army band coming closer and closer to the chapel. Then we heard the commands, the crisp clicking of heels and the snap of rifles bringing all to attention.

We watched as the pallbearers silently pushed Joel's flag-draped coffin down the long aisle to the front of the chapel. Our thoughts went back to Vietnam.

As I recounted the events of that day when Joel had been so brave, and as I told of his exploits, I found myself actually "there"—reliving with Joel and the men of the 173d all that had taken place that day.

For a time I lost the awareness of where I was and what I was doing, namely conducting Joel's funeral at Arlington Cemetery. I lost my place in the prepared notes and began to ramble. Although my wife knew something was wrong, she said at first it appeared that I was just very choked up over the occasion. But for me, I was actually transported in my mind back there to that hot, steamy jungle where life had hung on a thread for so many of us. I felt it all over as if it were happening again.

I was having a flashback, something that many combat soldiers have experienced. My wife hurried outside and stood beside me in the line after the service, whispering the names of people coming through the line. As one man approached, she coached me, "Tony is coming though the line."

I asked her, "Who is Tony?"

"Your best friend," she said. I did not really "come back" until later that evening and it was the only time I ever experienced such a vivid and all-consuming flashback. It gave me a personal understanding of what many of our fighting soldiers have experienced.

Hill 65 will be etched in my memory forever, as it most certainly will for all those who were there. The awards and decorations were numerous. Our unit, the 1st Battalion (Airborne) 503rd Infantry received the Presidential Distinguished Unit Citation, the highest award our country gives to any of its military units. Specialist Joel received the Congressional Medal of Honor. Captain Tucker and his First Sergeant, Edgar Board received the Distinguished Service Cross; Lieutenant Colonel Tyler received the Silver Star, I received the Bronze Star with "V" device for valor. On and on it went.

Hill 65 was a harrowing experience, but it reconfirmed for many of us the truth of God's sovereign watch-care over His own. Psalm 91 became a living reality for me in those days. As I wrote in *Beyond Combat*, a book about this year in Vietnam, I specifically learned that "there is no such thing as a bullet that has written on it, 'To Whom It May Concern.'" People who should have died did not, and people in seeming safe places were killed. Only God, the Sovereign Lord, knows the answer to all these questions, but I did find great faith and hope and assurance in the promises of Psalm 91:

> *You shall not be afraid of the terror by night,*
> *Nor of the arrow that flies by day.*
> *Nor of the pestilence that walks in darkness,*
> *Nor of the destruction that lays waste at noonday.*
>
> *A thousand may fall at your side,*
> *And ten thousand at your right hand;*
> *But is shall not come near you.*
> *He will give his angels charge over you,*
> *To keep you in all your ways.*

CHAPTER 3

After Vietnam: Recovery and Reassignment

As soon as I could, I called Patty and told her I had been wounded, but assured her that everything was going to be all right. After what we had just been through, just to hear her voice was a soothing comfort as well as a reassuring, emotional lift. Lord, how I loved that woman. How I missed her and longed to hold her again. How I missed my little children. When she put them on the phone to tell Daddy they loved him, it was as if they were in the next room. My heart was blessed and broken at the same time.

Most of the recovery time was spent at the 1st Field Hospital in Saigon. Surgery had been performed at the 3rd MASH (Mobile Army Surgical Hospital) in Ben Hoa, the base camp of the 173d Airborne Brigade. There the bullet had been removed, necessary incisions and sutures made, and I was sent for recuperation to the First Field Hospital in Saigon.

During that stay I had a lot of time to think and pray, time for serious soul-searching and reevaluation. This near-death experience caused me to think more seriously about how I should spend the rest of my life. Certainly God was in the equation. I wanted to serve Him and be in the center of His will, but what did that mean? I recall having a strong sense or impression that this episode was a prelude to something else, that somehow it was part of something else God had for the future.

Israel was always swimming around in thoughts and possible scenarios for the future. Nothing was clear at that point, but Israel had remained gentle on my mind as an ever-present reality. I remember laying there in the hospital in Vietnam, turning to the maps in the back of my Bible, studying the map of Israel and imagining myself being there. But, in what capacity? What would I do there?

There seemed to be no way to get there from where I was, and from the way God had so obviously led up to now. I had returned to the Army as a Chaplain, thinking that was what God had for me for a career. Now, for the first time since I had returned to the Army, I began to think there might be something else God had for us outside and beyond the Army.

Frankly, it was a little unsettling to even consider these things, since we both loved the Army and ministry in the military. At this point I had not even shared these thoughts with Patty. I felt no push to make a decision at that time, especially in light of the need to get healed and back on my feet. For the time being, I decided to let the Army take its course and see what would happen.

On January 1, 1966, I was well enough to go out on our unit's next operation. Although still limping and tiring very easily, I definitely was ready to return to the field with the troops. Here was where I felt I belonged and was needed—with the soldiers where the action was, literally and spiritually. And that was where I spent the rest of my tour in Vietnam until I returned in July of 1966.

Coming Home

Only someone who has been in extended, bloody combat knows the joy of being back in the States and reunited with family. This was the greatest thrill of all. Yet there was a type of culture shock in returning to America after spending the previous year in the jungles of Vietnam.

It took major adjustments. I remember when Patty picked me up at O'Hare Airport in Chicago. Although she drove only about 35—40 mph in the far right line on the freeway, I kept telling her, "Slow down, Patty. Slow down." I hadn't moved that fast in a year. Also, while I was gone for a year, Patty had managed everything, including the house, the car, the yard, the finances and the children. In fact, she had done an excellent job alone. Now I was back and there would be necessary re-divisions of labor and responsibility in the family. We slowly made changes without major problems; still it took adjustments for all of us.

One of those adjustments was living on a military post again. I was assigned at Fort Bragg, North Carolina to the 6th Special Forces Group (The Green Berets). As a chaplain in Vietnam, on several occasions I had conducted services in Special Forces camps. Now I was going to be one of them. Indeed, it was an honor and a privilege to serve with these men, the most highly trained and professional soldiers in the U.S. Army.

After two years with the 6th Special Forces Group at Fort Bragg, I was transferred to Fort Devens, Massachusetts, to serve with the 10th Special Forces Group, a unit that had just returned from Germany. This was a wonderful tour in every way. Soon after we checked in and moved in to our quarters at Ft. Devens, our third child Rachel was born on August 10, 1968. Also, I had the glad duty of organizing and establishing a new chapel, "The Liberator's Chapel," named after the Special Forces motto "De Oppresso Liber," to liberate the oppressed—certainly a fitting title with obvious spiritual overtones.

It was at Fort Devens, however, that I sensed my first clear guidance regarding Israel. It was a long time in coming, but it was now upon us and it was going to require a major decision. Patty has always been a vital part of the decision making in our home and before I get into what the actual decision involved, I want you to hear from her about the journey of faith that we had experienced together up to this point.

Patty's Perspective

It's difficult to go from today, back through our life in Israel, then even further back to Vietnam days because of something like a huge, invisible wall between then and now. Yet, as I looked back to remember how I ever got involved with Israel in the first place, I have tried in vain to recall the first time I heard the word *Israel* as referring to a present-day people. I vaguely remember sitting around the little radio in our home and hearing about the end of World War II, primarily because the family was excited and said that my older brother Buddy would be coming home from the war. And later in 1948, I was too young to grasp the significance of the establishment of the State of Israel, although at some point after that event, I recall seeing charts in church explaining the Book of Revelation and the end times. There, Israel was always front and center.

Still later we were taught that Gog and Magog in Revelation was Russia, an evil, anti-God, Communist empire and that Russia and nations from the East were going to attack Israel one day. But not to worry, because just when it looks like all is gone, Jesus will return and wipe out the enemies of Israel and establish His Kingdom on earth. Somehow we understood we would also be a part of that.

But **Israelites!** Now that was something else. I have tried in vain to remember when I did *not* know that word. Everyone I knew, knew the Israelites. They were God's Chosen People. They were the Victors in battle. They were brought out of Egypt by Moses. They went in and conquered the Holy Land that God swore to them. They were the ones who always came through because they had Jehovah on their side. And I knew early on that if I wanted victory in my life, it was that same God of Israel who would bring it about.

The Israelites included Abraham, Isaac, Jacob, Moses, Daniel, Elijah, Solomon, King David, Isaiah, Jeremiah, and Ezekiel, all heroes of mine. The Israelites were the people who preserved God's Word or "The Good Book," which, according to Mama, I had better make sure I hid in my heart so that I would not sin against God. The 10 Commandments were as etched in my mind and heart as they were on those stones in Sinai. Israelites included all the apostles and disciples. And most important of all, the Israelites produced the Lion of the Tribe of Judah, the Living Word, Jesus Christ.

Although there was only one Jewish family in my small, Southern hometown, and they were friends, it simply never occurred to me to dislike Jews. In fact, somewhere in my psyche was implanted an abiding love for Jews, Israel, Israelites and anything related.

One of the first lectures I ever heard came from my mother, whom I discovered years later in genealogical studies had some Jewish ancestors 15 generations back. Mama always preceded something important with, "Now Patty, you can remember this or you can forget it!" Then she would tell me something very, very big.

About the time of the establishment of the State of Israel, she stood right in front of me one day with a stern, prophet-kind-of-look—the sort of look the preacher sometimes had when he was warning people about hell.

She then said, "Now Patty, you can remember this or you can forget it! The Good Book says that if you bless Abraham, you will be blessed, and if you curse Abraham, you will be cursed. Do you understand?"

At that time I did not have the slightest clue as to what she meant, but I did think well of Abraham and so I told her, "Yes ma'am. I understand. I will remember."

And I did and I do remember. From that time as a young girl until I went to Wheaton College there was little input that differed from my early learning. Even in college I don't recall anyone ever making negative statements about Jews. In fact, comments about Israel were usually very positive. Our college was one of many colleges and universities that sent students to study in Israel and even as today, many people referred to that land as the Holy Land.

My third year in college had come and I was thinking that I would go into Young Life work with high school students. Then I met Jim. Although I cannot really say that I understand today any better than then exactly how love happens, when I met Jim Hutchens, it happened. I found out that he had seen me in several places on campus, but when I met him at Freddie's, a little store near campus, I was seriously impressed at first sight. He was just back from two years in the Army with the 11th Airborne Division. He had a white-sidewall haircut and big, muscular, tanned arms bulging out of his rolled-up khaki shirtsleeves. When one of my Ivy-League-ish girlfriends asked me if Jim had anything to wear but those Army clothes, I snapped back, "I sure hope not!"

Not being given to timidity, I no doubt gave it away, but within no more than two weeks, I was sure this was the man for me. In fact, although it is somewhat embarrassing to admit it, I actually told him, "I think I am in love with you." He paused a few moments and then said he would have to pray about it. I sensed that this was not his usual approach with girls in his former life before coming to faith, and I was willing to wait. The very next day he came back, told me he had prayed about it and that he loved me, too.

Soon after, we went to my hometown of Winnfield, Louisiana, with the goal of getting the approval of my parents. My daddy instantly liked Jim because he was a man's man, offered him a choice piece of land on the farm and even promised to build us a nice house. Mama was happy, because he loved Jesus and that was all there was to it.

The whole future lay before us then and with his decision to go for the Army Chaplaincy, we finished college and headed for seminary in Dallas, Texas. I taught high school and he studied. When I was pregnant with our first child and was required to quit teaching at 5 months, I started typing theses for pay and got a part time job helping to write, do art work and to co-star in a children's TV show in Dallas called "Charles and Miss Patty."

On November 22, 1963, I was coming back from an OBGYN appointment in the Parkland Hospital area and turned onto the road under the overpass in downtown Dallas, going toward our house on Live Oak Street. While under that bridge, I began to hear loud noises, piercingly blaring sirens, and shouts. Almost immediately at least two dozen policemen on huge motorcycles began to whiz by me, now 7 months pregnant, and Matt, our little 18-month old boy who was in a little car seat to my right. I pulled over to the right side of the road until they finally passed and then cautiously began to creep along on the side of the grassy knoll, across the street from the Dallas Book Depository.

Although I was somewhat frightened because of the children, I had no idea that the President of the United States had just been shot less than 100 yards away. As I drove through Dallas I noticed people running wildly, screaming and crying. I knew that the President was in Dallas that day, and my first thoughts were that this was a very extreme reaction to seeing the President in a parade. Not until I finally drove into our little apartment and Jim came running out to meet me, did I have any idea of the horrible tragedy we had literally driven by. I realized that if indeed there was a conspiracy, the shooter could have easily gotten away in a car— and that car could have been mine.

After that tragic day, Jim went to a local store and bought a pistol. I began to stockpile food and fill the bathtub up with water every night before going to bed. In the missile-crisis, cold war, and troubled years that followed, we found ourselves even more eager to move toward the military.

Sarah, our second baby, was born two months later - just a few months before Jim got orders to report to Ft. Campbell, Kentucky as an Army Chaplain. We settled into housing on the post. Thinking that we would have a career in the Army for the next twenty-five to thirty years, I may have been the happiest woman alive. Even Vietnam did not dampen this spirit of love for the military and the place God had called me as an Army Chaplain's wife. I had absolutely no clue about what would follow in the years to come.

Vietnam from a Distance

Weeks before Jim left for Vietnam, we lived every day thinking it might be our last together for a long time. Many times his unit was alerted and he would pack up all his gear, kiss us all goodbye and head for wherever it was that they went to wait. And there were no cell phones in those days. So we just tried to go on with normal life and be calm.

Finally, one day I was in the commissary getting our groceries and went through the line where a sergeant's wife I knew was the checkout lady. We chatted a moment or two and then she leaned over to whisper to me, "They are leaving for sure on Wednesday." (I can't remember the day of the week she told me so I will just say Wednesday)

I hugged her and went on home. When Jim came home that evening I told him what someone had told me that day, although I did not tell him her name. I knew that her husband would be in deep trouble if it were ever traced to him. Jim immediately called his commanding officer and said, "Sir, someone told Patty today that we are leaving Wednesday."

When his commander asked, "Who was it?" Jim answered, "She won't say, sir."

The commander continued, "Chaplain, she's right, but

you are not to tell a single other person."

"Yes sir," Jim said and hung up. And Wednesday it was. Let me quote from *Beyond Combat*, a book he later wrote about his experience in Vietnam, what Jim wrote about our last day.

> *On the eve of my departure the children sensed that this was our last day together. We spent a quiet evening enjoying each other. Matt and I walked over to a Little League ball game and had some cokes and popcorn. We went home and played games together, and then it was time for bed. That night we spent a little longer than usual "talking to Jesus." Matt asked Him to take care of Daddy; Sarah mumbled something only she and God understood; and then they both went off to sleep.*
>
> *At three the next morning everyone rolled out. Patty planned to get an early start in order to meet the movers in Wheaton by mid-day. At three thirty she was ready to leave.*
>
> *Those few moments are stamped forever on my memory. I can still feel the emptiness that swept over me, the creeping aloneness that only the companionship of one's family can dispel, the helplessness and uncertainty that persisted as I considered an unknown and hostile future.*
>
> *Not given to tears, I found they came quite easily as I hugged and kissed my children and remembered that it would be a year before I held them again... A year—if ever. As for Patty, she kept her tears for the long, anxious months ahead.*

Actually, as we drove away and I watched through the rearview mirror as the children kept waving to their Daddy, I nearly bit off a chunk of lip trying not to cry in front of the children. But moments later, as we turned a corner and Jim was gone, while Matt just sat there staring out the window, Sarah asked, "Mommy, are we going to cry?"

That was it. I said, "Yes, darling, we are going to cry." All three of us starting crying. Our first stop was just moments down the road to get our first diversion—a Coke with a straw for each of us.

We finally made it to Wheaton where we had rented a small house near the college. I cannot imagine why I allowed this to happen, but we had given the movers permission to get the key from the owner and move our things in. When we got there, it was bedlam. Things were thrown all over the house, and boxes had been opened and pilfered through. I never even really knew what all was stolen. Since the year was so difficult anyway the last thing I worried about was what was missing from our household goods.

I never found a very expensive watch Jim's mother had been given him for graduation from Seminary. They also stole a beautiful antique clock from Germany that was a gift from some friends who had been stationed there, as well as many other items that could be grabbed easily. I have often wondered what happened to those men, knowing they had robbed a young mother with small children, a young wife whose husband was gone for a year in a bloody war.

On the bright side, however, I was rescued by a couple who had been best of friends since Dallas, Texas days. Bobby Hopkins was an All-American basketball player from the West, and he and his wife Donna Jean came to be with me the first 10 days Jim was gone. We called them "Nabes." They had been married 15 years and had no children, so they were free to pick up and help out a damsel in distress.

And "help out" is not an adequate term. Bob taught math

and physics and was a genius at just about everything. He repaired everything in the house, installed the washer and dryer, and checked everything from the chimney to the wiring. The last time I looked the fireplace had been filled with about three to four inches of cigarette butts and the next time I looked it was spotless. He checked all the windows for safety locks and literally set up my whole house for a year. Donna Jean unpacked every dish and with Bob, every book and item in our house. They organized every nook and cranny in every room. They insisted on cooking dinner and doing the dishes and in the evenings they went for long walks with the children, cheerfully talking and laughing.

By the time they left, I was better settled and organized than I have ever been in any house and felt much more confident about the coming year. Because they had such a wonderful time with Matt and Sarah and so enjoyed children, after 15 years of having none, they went home and adopted a little girl. As is often the case, in a short period of time Donna got pregnant and they had a second little girl. That was one of the good results of the Vietnam War, and they have remained treasured friends until this day.

Another wonderful surprise awaited me in the couple who lived next door. The man was at least 6 feet, 6 inches tall and very friendly and protective during the whole year. His wife was attentive and quite compassionate. He had gone off to World War II "for the duration" while she was pregnant and had come home over five years later to a little girl who didn't know him. In light of their prolonged experience in war, I was hesitant to complain about anything that whole year.

The Army wives had been briefed and warned before we left post that many people were harassing wives of men in Vietnam. Sure enough, I got calls and people showed up at the door to be ugly. Many times, I just called my friend next door and he would come through the back way and answer my front door. One day a very suspicious man came to the door and asked me if my husband got sent to Vietnam with a certain unit. He said, "I see you have a sticker from Ft. Campbell, Kentucky."

I sensed he was up to no good and I simply whispered, "No, sir, he wishes he were. He got stuck up in the R.O.T.C department of this dinky little college here in town." So he left and never came back. Occasionally when my neighbor wasn't home and I had to have a delivery made to my house, I would enlist either Richard Gross or Don Beless, friends from college days who lived nearby to be my "husband" of the day.

Because of what we were seeing on television by then about the war and because of harassment problems, I nailed shut every window in the house. I especially made sure that no one could get in through a basement window. Not only were there several large nails in each window, but I put furniture or boards across the windows too so that it would have taken a hammer and lots of noise to get in any window in our house. At least twice each day I went outside with the children. We went for a walk, played in the yard, or drove to the store, the library, or the military post on the North Shore of Chicago. Around 4:30 in the afternoon, we were back in the house with every window and door locked up tight. Until bedtime, we played games, read stories, did craft projects or read.

One day when I was watching the news about the war, I heard that Jim's unit had been ambushed. In the early days of the Vietnam War the media would broadcast by name which units were on operations and even where they would be. Fortunately they stopped doing that about a year into the war, but that day the reporter announced that many had been killed and wounded in Jim's unit. I had received a letter a day or two before telling me they would be in a particular war zone on a specific day. This was the day and that was the war zone. Now I knew for sure his unit had been badly hit.

We had been told at Ft. Campbell that if our man was killed or wounded, we would usually be notified within 48 hours. Normally, two officers would show up at the door to personally and officially notify you that your husband was killed. For unmarried soldiers, they notified parents. Women used to watch with shock and awe as a military car slowly drove down the street while everyone watched in fear to see which driveway it would turn in. If it were your house, you knew what was coming. If a neighbor's house, the others immediately ran out to be with them. Now I was in a town without military companions around me, so I watched alone while trying to act normal in front of the children.

I talked with Jim by phone only two or three times in the whole year he was gone and I knew this would not be one of those times. With no way to find out anything, we simply had to go on with life. We listened to cassette tapes of Daddy's voice as we had each day and waited it out. After three days passed I began to feel some relief. When the fourth day came to a close, I was able to get a good night's sleep and began to take heart that Jim was probably alive.

Two very long weeks later, I got a short letter from Jim saying that he had been wounded, but that he was all right. He had asked the military not to notify me since he judged it would be better to wait and tell me himself. Indeed he had been shot and all of them lay in the jungle for a whole day hoping to be rescued. With heavy blood loss, some didn't make it, but Jim had been patched up enough by Medic Lawrence Joel and was flown out by helicopter the next day. General Ellis Williamson had braved continuing enemy fire to lead the rescue efforts for his men. That was in early November. As soon as Jim was able, January 1, 1966 to be exact, he went back out to the front with his men and didn't return to the States until the next summer. It was a long year.

Every day I wrote a very long letter to Jim and mailed it to Vietnam. A couple of years later I met a Catholic

Chaplain who had been with Jim that entire year, and he thanked me for all the letters I wrote. I looked rather dumbfounded, and he told me that Jim let him read parts of his letters every day. He said they had been a beautiful gift to him during a very lonely year.

Jim sent short notes as often as he could and I stored them away for safe keeping after reading parts of them to the children. A few times he sent little reel-to-reel audiotapes. The first time I played one Matt didn't realize exactly what it was, and thought his daddy was talking live to him.

Jim would say, "Hi Matt, how are you son?"

Matt would answer, "Daddy, is that you?"

"Are you playing nicely with your sister Sarah?"

"Daddy, where are you? Can you come out?"

"Sarah, how's my little baby girl?"

"Mommy, where is daddy?" Matt would ask and look over at me. Finally, he learned to just listen, knowing that the words were only one way. I was determined that the children would remember their daddy that year, so every day we listened to his voice.

Once Matt asked me if he could have a toy gun he saw in the store. I told him we would have to write Daddy and ask if it was okay. So that day I wrote a letter, put it in an envelope and together we went out to the mailbox and put it in with the flag up. While they were napping, I got the letter, wrote another one from Jim and put it in the mailbox to retrieve after they woke up from naps. And of course, for almost everything they asked for in letters that year, Daddy said, "Yes."

Those Vietnam days are as real for us today as they were then. For the men and women who went and bore the pain and suffering of war, we owe a great debt of gratitude. While many people back at home rioted and fought louder and meaner about our troops being there, and while some politicians either knowingly lied or misled the nation, and while a few famous Hollywood types made fools of themselves, nearly 60,000 people gave their lives for us.

My husband was nearly one of them. I argue and disagree with Jim on many things, but every time I look at his face, I see a brave soldier who was willing to serve his country without whining. I see a man whom I respect and honor. And I often quote to him the Bible words that God spoke to Israel, "Oh Ephraim, Ephraim, though I often speak against you, still I remember you, I have great compassion for you and my heart yearns for you."

General Jim, my man, I'm proud of you. I salute you!

CHAPTER 4
Marching to Zion

Dr. Young Comes to Boston

It was late January, 1969. I had just returned from the White Mountains of New Hampshire where the 10th Special Forces had been conducting several weeks of winter ski training. No matter where you go, it's always good to get home and Patty and the children were indeed welcome sights. Rachel, the newest addition to our family as of August 10, 1968, was beginning to recognize me with little smiles reserved just for Daddy.

Soon after unpacking, I went into the kitchen where Patty was preparing dinner. With one hand still stirring a pot of vegetable soup, she reached out with the other and handed me a recent edition of the Boston Globe with a small article she had encircled. "Take a look at this article," she said. "I thought you might be interested."

The brief article was about one Dr. G. Douglas Young, who headed a school on Mount Zion in Israel called The American Institute of Holy Land Studies. The article said that Dr. Young had received a Ph.D. from Dropsie College of Hebrew and Cognate Learning and that he had formerly served as the Dean and Professor of Old Testament Languages and Interpretation at Trinity Evangelical Seminary in Deerfield, Illinois. He had founded the

American Institute in 1959 with the goal of providing either a short or long term "Israel Experience" of academic training for students from a consortium of Christian schools, colleges and seminaries.

Both Wheaton College and Dallas Theological Seminary were among the members of the consortium. The article said there was to be a reception for Dr. Young in downtown Boston and that he would be speaking of the opportunities that the American Institute offered. Anyone who was interested was invited to attend. I was definitely interested.

When I first returned from Vietnam, I had applied for the Army's FAS (Foreign Area Studies) Program, an excellent program where one is trained as a specialist in a certain area of the world, to include extensive language training. Of course, my area of interest was the Middle East, especially Israel. To my dismay, I found that at that time, the *only* branch of service that could *not* attend the FAS program was the Chaplains' branch. With our involvement in that region today and for the foreseeable future, such restrictions may be removed but in any case, although that door was shut, personal interest in Israel continued. Now I wondered if the American Institute might in some way serve to fulfill the same motivations that led me to seek the Army's FAS program. As I later drove in from Ft.Devens to Boston to attend that meeting, I hoped that Dr. Young would have some answers or suggestions.

After Dr. Young's presentation, I went to him and asked if I could talk to him about the possibility of attending his school. I told him I was an active duty chaplain, a veteran of Vietnam, and was now serving with the 10th Special Forces at Ft.Devens. Initially, my thought was to take a study leave of absence from the Army and attend the school for a year or two, although I was not sure if the Army would agree to that arrangement. In any case, Dr. Young had a completely different idea.

He suggested, "Since you have completed your under-graduate and seminary training, why don't you consider coming to the American Institute as our Chaplain?" He went on to tell of the Institute's need for a chaplain for the students, as well as the need for someone ordained to the ministry and trained to conduct church services and Bible studies for both students and staff. In addition, he said I could help him by teaching some courses. Since the Institute had working relationship with the Hebrew University, he sweetened the offer by saying I could take courses there and even work toward an additional degree.

Naturally, I raised the concern for finances and housing for my family. Dr. Young assured me there would be sufficient salary for one year and that we could re-evaluate after that time. He then offered me a package that would include off-campus housing and said, "Why don't you think about it and pray about it with your wife? Let's think in terms of one year, with a possibility of extending your stay." I told him I would do just that and would get back to him. Since he was planning to be in the States for six more weeks, I planned to check with the Army to see if a leave of absence could be granted. At least he would have my response by the time his stay in the States was completed.

Driving back to Ft. Devens, my head was swimming non-stop. On the one hand, this was an incredible opportunity! On the other, it would require a huge change for the whole family. We *really* needed the Lord's wisdom and guidance. That evening as I related the meeting and the offer to Patty, I could see she had reservations and many questions relating to family that would have to be answered if this came about. For me, the first and most obvious question was how the Army Chaplains' Branch would respond?

That didn't take long to find out. I called the Chief of Chaplains' office the next day and asked them if a leave of absence was possible, explaining the purposes Dr. Young had outlined. Although leaves of absence were granted for graduate studies, they said the kind of arrangement Dr. Young was suggesting, unfortunately, did not meet the requirements. The Chief's office was very understanding of my interests and desires, but Army regulations and the Chief of Chaplains' guidelines simply made it out of the question. That posed a real problem. What to do?

As Patty and I talked and prayed about it, what had previously been unthinkable for both of us began to surface as a live option—but how could we actually leave the Army?

To say that this decision produced unwanted and ever-present stress for us both is putting it mildly. I had been greatly blessed as an Army chaplain, having risen in rank from a First Lieutenant to a Major in only five years. Although rapid promotions are not uncommon during times of war, I had been blessed each time with promotion on what is called the "5% list," that is, from the top 5% of those eligible for promotion. I had been chosen to receive a Regular Army commission and had experienced great favor with my commanders and with the troops I had served.

I had been asked to write a book (*Beyond Combat*) about my Vietnam experience and it had sold over 100,000 copies. I was even featured in Time magazine as an example and model of a combat chaplain in Vietnam. The Chief of Chaplains' office had treated me well and some commanders under whom I had served actually encouraged me to believe that I might someday be the Chief of Chaplains. It seemed as though no matter what life brought our way in those days, it was accompanied by enormous blessings. It's not easy to give up this kind of favor and blessing. It is downright gut wrenching to leave "this man's Army" when it's part of your lifeblood. If we were to leave the Army, I had to be sure, really sure that this was God's will. This was to be one serious decision.

Still, in the midst of it all, Israel tugged heavily on my

heartstrings. Here was an opportunity to minister and study in the "Promised Land." We're talking about the place where Jesus lived, died, and rose from the dead. We're talking about the place where Jesus promised He would one day return, the Holy Land where it all started and where history, as we know it, will reach its climax. Then, even as today, the eyes of the world were on Jerusalem.

It had been about a week since speaking with Dr. Young and by now, he had five weeks left before he returned to Israel. I had promised to get back to him with a decision before he left the country and time seemed to be flying. Patty and I agreed to pray and seek the counsel of others for the next two to three weeks before we made the decision. During that time a vision of ministry in Israel was growing. It was as though I was being wooed toward Israel with an ever increasing longing and a desire to be there and be a part of what God was doing now and what He would be doing in the future.

With Patty and me, there was a growing sense that somehow we belonged there, that we were supposed to be a part of what God was going to do in Israel. The counsel I sought was mixed—some encouraged us to go; others reminded me of the blessings I had received in the Army. We increasingly felt desperate to hear from the Lord.

Looking back, I'm not sure when I personally moved from questions to answers, but at the end of this time of seeking God's direction, it just seemed the right thing to do. I would get out of the Army and we would go to Israel. Next to my decisions to follow Jesus Christ and to marry Patty, this was my biggest decision ever. I prayed I was right.

Out of the Army—On to Israel

I contacted Dr. Young and told him of my decision. He was delighted and assured me that he would do everything he could to make our move as smooth as possible. I told him that it would take time to process out of the Army and that I had set July 31ˢᵗ as my target date for release, which would put us in Israel in time for the fall semester. He agreed that would be a good starting time, so I began to make the necessary preparations to get out of the Army and go to Israel. Now it was a matter of checklists. We were actually going. All the dreams and imaginations that arose from studying about Israel, all the visions of the Promised Land I had heard and even preached and taught about would be experienced. We would see all the places on the maps in the back of the Bible. We would not just see them; we would live there. It was exciting.

Good-byes

The Army knows how to say goodbye. It's done thousands of times all over the world every day. Sometimes the good-byes are tragically to a family of a soldier killed in action and sometimes it is just to a soldier with orders for his next assignment at another military post. There is the normal round of good-bye get-togethers, dinners, awards and banquets. In what my wife called our "Airborne, Green Beret, 10ᵗʰ Special Forces, Alligator Eating Congregation," or *The Liberators Chapel* as it was listed in the weekly bulletin, I was presented with a beautiful handmade plaque.

Other chaplains with whom we had been serving gave us a special farewell party and the senior chaplain invoked God's blessings on us for future ministry. The 10ᵗʰ Special Forces Commander and officers gave us a uniquely designed plaque and awarded me the Meritorious Service Medal. Major Alton "Butch" Baker, a 10ᵗʰ Special Forces medical doctor and close family friend, gave us a bag of medicines and a vaccination shot for every disease possible in the Middle East. It was a bittersweet farewell. But, now it was on to Israel. The words of Adoniram Judson came to mind, "The future is as bright as the promises of God."

In Flight

We flew out of JFK airport on August 1, 1969, first to France and then on to Lod Airport just outside Tel Aviv. By now, the whole family was excited. I was pumped. Since the first leg of the flight was at night, we had gotten a prescription of Dramamine to help the older two children sleep better. It didn't work. They were in fact "wired," probably partly because they were leaving a place they loved and partly in anticipation of going to the Land where Jesus lived.

When we got to Paris, we had to change planes for the last leg to Israel and as we walked to our next flight, our son Matt had trouble walking straight. As a matter of fact, our seven-year-old son wobbled and chuckled his way through the entire airport. Since the passersby didn't know about the Dramamine, their looks of disdain at my wife and me said it all, "How could you be so cruel to a child as to allow him to get drunk?"

During the four-hour flight from Paris to Tel Aviv, we finally were able to get some rest but the excitement and anticipation of actually going to Israel kept us from any deep sleep. For me, it was hard to believe that we were really going to be living and working in the "Promised Land."

The American Institute of Holy Land Studies

Jim Monson, the second-in-command at the American Institute of Holy Land Studies, met us at the Lod Airport in Israel. In fact, we were to live on the first floor of the house he and his wife owned on Rehov HaRakevet, "The Street of the Train," where twice a day a train from Tel Aviv to Jerusalem went by on the tracks running parallel to the street. It was an old stone house with high ceilings that kept it cool in summer, but damp and cold in winter. It was a delightful place in south Jerusalem in a wonderful neighborhood in the heart of what is called the German Colony. Within a week, Patty's artistic touch made it look and feel like home.

It was a place, however, that served to remind us on a regular basis of the deep wounds and scars left on some Israelis from their death camp experiences. Across the street from us lived an elderly woman, a Holocaust survivor who had the tattooed numbers on her arm as a living reminder. Often during the day we would see her out and about in her yard. Then days would go by with no one seeing her. Sometimes, seemingly out of nowhere, would come blood-curdling, horrific screams, screams of anguish, of fear and pain. She was reliving the nightmarish horrors of Auschwitz. We were told that there was nothing anyone could do for her other than befriend her on her good days.

At Lod airport, we had crammed our family of five and all our belongings into Jim's little powder blue Volkswagen station wagon. As we drove the 35 miles from Lod Airport up the winding, mountainous road to Jerusalem, I could feel my heart pounding within me. What a privilege—what a thrill to actually be in this land, I thought. Somehow, I felt this was my home, the home I never had, even though I had never even seen this place before. I felt this was where I was supposed to be. Even then, I was ready to spend the rest of my life in Israel. However, it was not in God's providential plan for us to stay at that time.

Even as I write these words in the 21st Century, some 34 years later, I still feel the same way about Israel. It's the home of my heart. The longing is still there. No doubt, countless Christians have felt the same way as they have made pilgrimages there. Most certainly, the Jews that God has been re-gathering to the Land, just as He promised He would, know that same feeling of finally having arrived home.

These "Exiles" whom God has been restoring to the land since its rebirth in 1948 have made that same trek to Jerusalem. Like they, we could see the burned-out remains of trucks and half-tracks that have been left as memorials to the Jewish people's struggle for independence and national sovereignty. It is a living testimonial to God's faithfulness to His ancient covenants to Abraham, the Patriarchs and their descendants, the Jews of today. Indeed, the fact that Israel became a nation on May 14, 1948, under its own sovereign control for the first time since the Babylonian captivity in 586 BC, is nothing short of a miracle of God. That is especially true in light of the forces that have been arrayed against her from the beginning, with Arab aggression preventing peace since Israel's birth.

There was no attempt on the part of the Arabs to deny they started the 1948 war. Jamal Hussieini admitted this when he told the U. N. Security Council on April 16, 1948,

> "The representative of the Jewish Agency told us yesterday that they were not the attackers, that the Arabs had begun the fighting. *We do not deny this.* We told the whole world that we were going to fight."

General John Bagot Glubb, the British commander of Jordan's Arab Legion, likewise admitted the Arabs initiated the fighting. Listen to his own words:

> "Early in January, the first detachments of the Arab *Liberation* Army began to infiltrate into Palestine from Syria. Some came through Jordan and even through Amman ... They were in reality to strike the first blow in the ruin of the Arabs in Palestine."

Finally, when the five Arab armies (Egypt, Syria, Transjordan, Lebanon and Iraq) invaded Israel, their intentions were declared by the Secretary-General of the Arab

League, Azzam Pasha: "This will be a war of extermination and a momentous massacre which will be spoken of like the Mongolian massacres and the Crusades." [Mitchell G. Bard, *Myths and Facts: A Guide to the Arab-Israeli Conflict*, American-Israeli Cooperative Enterprise: 2002, page 39]. Looking back on all the wars of Israel since 1948, they all started the same with Arab hate-filled aggression and they all ended the same with an Israeli victory. Certainly, Israel's victories, spectacular as they have been against odds up to 50 to 1, could not have happened if the Lord of Hosts (Armies) had not intervened on their behalf.

This thought of the Lord of Hosts coming to Israel's rescue kept running through my mind that day in 1969 as we crept ever closer to Jerusalem and to a new calling as Chaplain at the American Institute of Holy Land Studies. I knew that I, too, would need God to intervene on my behalf if this ministry was to be anything near what God wanted.

The American Institute of Holy Land Studies, as it was known then (since renamed The Jerusalem University College), had actually started in 1959 in a Christian and Missionary Alliance Church on the Street of the Prophets in downtown Jerusalem. Dr. Young, along with his devoted wife Georgina (affectionately called Snook), moved the Institute to Mount Zion in the summer of 1967. But let Snook tell you about that.

One day, when Doug was looking around the city, he saw the former Bishop Gobat School, situated on the edge of No-Man's Land just below the Old City wall and Zion Gate - on the southern slopes of Mt. Zion! This building had not been occupied since 1948, almost 20 years. It was just a shell.

However, it was still on the Jerusalem-Israel side and could be reached by climbing the pathway to David's Tomb. The beautiful ascent to Mt. Zion, as we have it today, was not yet built.

The road around Mt. Zion, then called the Pope's Road because it had been repaired for the visit of the Pope to Jerusalem, was not used for public travel (because of the dangers of snipers on the other side of the border), except for the few people who lived on Mt. Zion near David's Tomb.

This lovely building, standing empty for so long, cried out to be used, to be restored once again, as a school and a center. This surely was the right building to be the new home of the American Institute! What a beautiful setting, with the Judean Hills in the background, overlooking the Hinnom Valley. After much negotiation with the Archbishop of the Anglican Church who owned the property, the Government of Israel, and the army, permission was granted to take over the building of some 60 rooms and to restore it to its original building. It had been a boy's school up until 1948.

During the War of Independence, it was also headquarters for Israeli soldiers. At one time, the soldiers were completely cut off here and finally devised a way to get food and medicines into the building by setting up a cable that ran from the Gobat school across the valley to the St. John's eye hospital on the other side (today's Alexander's restaurant). The cable was lowered before *dawn and raised again after dusk, so it wouldn't be detected. That area has now been designated as a war memorial.*

In the Spring of 1967, we were permitted to go up and start renovating the grounds and the buildings. ...In August of 1967, we moved our school to its new quarters on Mt. Zion. There was still much to be done, but we were able to move in without electricity and water, but that soon was to come. What a beautiful place to be looking at Jerusalem at sunrise and sunset, truly a City of Gold. The Judean Hills with all their beauty and the Old City nestled there in all its antiquity. Our school grew from 16 students to over 400, but not all at once. Different programs were set up to attract students from abroad. With our summer short-term program, we were able to care for 100 at a time. Our long-term program, one year, was smaller.

What an experience living on Mt. Zion with its history and its meaning for Jews and Christians. Isaiah 2:3 says: "For out of Zion shall go forth the law and the Word of the Lord from Jerusalem." Suddenly, from a borderline situation, we were in the center of everything. (From Snook's personal reminiscence, www.bridgesforpeace.org)

Now, only two years later, my family was coming to Mount Zion. We, too, felt like we were in the center of everything and beginning a new life. There is a saying in Hebrew, "Kol chadashot kashot," (All beginnings are difficult) but starting a chaplain's program from scratch was not new. With frequent moves in the Army and certainly in the war in Vietnam, it seemed as though all assignments had been starting something new. So, immediately, I began to set up office hours, thumbtack a large Month-at-a-Glance schedule behind my desk, and put together a complete program of services, Bible studies, and activities for students and staff.

There was one room in what seemed like the bowels of the Institute, partially carved out of the deep-down rock of Mount Zion. With newly whitewashed walls, this rock solid place was going to be the chapel. With a little creative "scrounging," as we called it in Vietnam, we came up with a pulpit, some candleholders, and a foot-pump organ that someone remarked may have come off Noah's Ark. After living in the Land of the Bible for even a short period of time, that idea didn't even seem far fetched. Someone collected sheets of praise songs and a few musty hymnals, and we were in business.

As for the teaching responsibilities, it was a honor and a privilege to be asked by Dr. Young to fill in for him as a kind of team teaching experience in a number of courses he taught. That made it possible to focus on some of the familiar biblical themes. At the same time, it afforded an opportunity to gain lasting insights from Dr. Young, a specialist in what could be called "Israelology," i.e. a focus on Israel from biblical, theological, social and political points of view. It was also a time for an immersion study program in conversational Hebrew, or Ulpan, as it called in Israel.

Although I did well with good grades in four years of biblical Hebrew in seminary, I was rather amazed that I could not speak a single sentence. Not so with Patty. Without any prior preparation, within days she was practicing everything she learned in Ulpan on real people. She went to the store often, and asked, "How do you say . . . ?" for everything she shopped for. She said, "Hello, how are you?" to everyone she met, made comments, and asked questions of everyone.

Patty sat down with kids in the streets to talk and learn and they loved it. She even took around little notes with phrases on them and pulled them out when needed. Privately, I kept thinking that some of this ability might be attributed to her being of the female persuasion, but most of it, I must admit, was hard work and a willingness to get out there and try without a the slightest fear of making mistakes.

Notice that I did not say, "Making a fool of her self." Years after, her efforts were rewarded by being selected to the National Scholastic Honor Society in Hebrew Studies. Even today, she does much of her devotional reading of the Bible in Hebrew and regularly studies and writes on the significance of the Hebrew letters.

Much of my time at the Institute, however, was spent with English speaking students. There was some counseling, but mostly I just interacted with them over what they were studying and what living in Israel was all about. Everyone had questions and many of them were the same questions asked today regarding the Israel/Arab/Palestinian conflict. These questions still remain unanswered and unresolved and probably will until the One comes who said, "I am making everything new" (Revelation 21:5).

More experiences lay ahead for us in our "Israeli Experience." Some would change us forever!

Patty's Perspective

This morning about 4:00 a.m.when I could not sleep and decided to start writing, I asked myself, "Why in the world would anyone get out of a comfortable bed in the middle of the night and write about pain? Who in the world would want to read about things I don't even want to remember, much less write about?"

That woman who had a family and lived with Chaplain Jim Hutchens in the world of the Army, way back at Ft.

Devens, doesn't really exist anymore. However, I reckoned there might be some value in sharing my journey so that other women could better know that their difficulties and trials are not uncommon.

The year Jim spent in Vietnam should have been a bad year for a wife living alone with two children, worrying every day about her husband getting shot ten thousand miles away. But it wasn't like that. Oh, sure, there were some lonely times, but there was never a day when I did not feel right about where we were, about what we were doing. Besides, I had learned from my mother to show up every day, to be thankful that I could work hard. I had learned not to complain. In fact, I had learned not to complain openly about anything.

Those days were what many people today call dysfunctional, perhaps especially so in the Deep South where I grew up. No one told anyone anything about anything at home, so when my dear Daddy came in the house wobbly and I asked what was wrong, Mama always said, "Nothing, honey, just go to bed." When my older brother got drunk and threatened to shoot us all, Mama just took the gun from him and said he didn't mean it.

When Granny and Grandpa and all the other loved ones died, we stood in front of the caskets and talked about how good they looked. Then we stayed all day, ate a lot of food when we weren't hungry and pretended everything was delicious, in fact, the best we had ever eaten. When some poor girl got pregnant in high school and went off to have the baby somewhere, no one said a word about babies. We just talked about how good it was of her to go to Houston to be with her Aunt Lucy who was dying and had no one to help. When she returned, no one asked any questions about the particulars. Later, in a sort of self-help group, when someone spoke about how, among other things, people in dysfunctional homes learn to lie, my first response was absolute denial. I had learned from my earliest days to smile, do what was right, be positive and make the best of every situation. Stuffing is what we call that today.

So when Jim came back from Vietnam and was restless and unsettled, I didn't think to connect it with either a year of guerrilla war in the jungles or the state of the world at that time. Many of our friends were even volunteering to go back early to Vietnam, even though riots and anti-war efforts were heating up. And always on the back burner of my mind was the Soviet Empire who threatened occasionally to "bury us." However, we were safe in the confines of a military post, God was still sovereign and my children were doing well.

When we moved from Ft. Bragg, North Carolina to Ft. Devens, Massachusetts and faced the worst winter blizzard in a century, with most of our men on ski training in the White Mountains of New Hampshire, I felt like a baby in her mother's arms because the Army took care of us. I knew that we were never going to be rich, but we were never going to alone either. It's hard for a non-military person to under-stand the love and commitment one can feel for the military life. Just driving in the post or base gate and being saluted brings a deep, personal sense of who you are and where you belong. Everyone knows what your rank is, what your salary is; and there are rules, which if followed, bring sure rewards. I was the ideal military wife. If it had been possible, I would have joined the Army myself, but that was only possible for women after my time.

Now my husband had taken a tiny, little article that I had given him to read and wanted to change our entire life. He wanted to get out of the Army? I would not allow myself to think he had lost his mind, but I began to understand for the first time that I was married to a man who jumped out of perfectly good airplanes. What was I to do?

Not being given to rebellion, and in fact, raised on fol-lowing the leadership of the husband, I was completely torn up inside. I judged that I could not talk to anyone about it, because *we* were the spiritual leaders, and besides that, I was trained from my youth to endure and never tell anyone anything about my personal struggles. Today I place that rule in the same place I put the one about not ever wearing dirty underwear in case you die and the undertaker sees it. The other option that looked large was that if we stayed in the Army, Jim would probably go back to Vietnam again and by now this thought didn't sound as right as it had before.

Then Jim suggested that we take a week vacation, go to Grandfather Mountain in North Carolina, camp out there, fast for a week and ask God to give us direction. That sounded very spiritual and biblical. Didn't Jesus say, "*When* you fast," not "*if* you fast?" If Jesus said it, I was willing to do it, and so off we went with a large tent and every conceivable tool and necessity for camping, all checked out from Army supplies. When we got to a quiet wooded area on Grandfather Mountain, Jim set up the campsite, spiked the tent down deep and dug a trench around it with an Army entrenching tool. He set up a kitchen area right outside the tent and a little private toilet area several yards away. Within a short period of time he had made a little home in the woods for his family. We had our big dog with us and I assumed that somewhere in the supplies was an Army pistol and whatever else we needed, so that night we crawled into our sleeping bags prepared for a great week.

Then morning came and the fast began. Well, the fast began for Jim and me, but of course, the kids had to eat. So while Jim read and prayed a lot, I cooked three square meals a day for the children while personally fasting. Of course, there was also the need for something for the children to do all day while Daddy was out seeking God's leading. I did every conceivable thing I could think of with the children in the woods and then began to load up the kids and drive to the nearest anything to look for something to do. After the first couple of days of fasting while preparing meals, the hunger pains subsided and I actually began to sense more value in what we were doing and began to quietly pray as the children played or took naps.

The very last day of the week came with no serious problems and Jim went out into the woods several hours for his last opportunity before going back to Ft. Devens. An hour or so after he walked off, Matt, our 7-year-old, wandered off a bit into the woods, but still in sight. I was sitting on a beach chair holding baby Rachel, with one eye on Matt and one eye on Sarah, who was content to play on a blanket near the tent.

All of a sudden, a huge brown bear wandered into our camping area and was actually reaching down with his paws to pull up one of the camp trashcans that were below ground. Quietly and with controlled panic as I put the girls in the back seat of the car, I called softly to Matt in the voice that he knew meant, "Do what I say and do it now." He ran immediately back to the tent and I looked him straight in the eye, "Son, get into the car this moment and do not get out. Now!"

With the children safe in the car and with both eyes on the bear now, I slowly dismantled the tent, packed our entire belongings, got inside, locked the doors and waited for Jim. It was a long wait. Naturally, right before Jim returned, the bear wandered off. When he returned and saw us packed and in the car, he came running over and asked, "What happened?" With that same sure look I'd given Matt, I stared at him, handed him the keys through a partially opened window and said, "We're going home. The fast is over."

Not only was the fast over, but in a short period of time we were on our way to Israel.

CHAPTER 5
Living Out Our Israeli Experience

A mong all our Israeli experiences, some of the most memorable were the field trips. The most memorable one began about ten days before Christmas in 1969, when I took twelve students on a field trip that was designed to retrace the trip the children of Israel took from Mount Sinai to the Promised Land, only in reverse order. Naturally comparing this trip to those recent days in the Army where I had served with some of the best and brightest soldiers in the world (Green Berets), I was really shocked to see how ill-prepared these kids were for anything even resembling a trek in the desert.

One lovely, young female student came dressed in a sleeveless blouse and wore beautiful red three-inch high heels. Another guy had only flip-flops for shoes. Most did not even have hats to protect them from the desert sun. Some brought chocolate, which, of course, would melt within minutes. I realized immediately that we would have to make some major adjustments in clothing and survival awareness, and I found myself in an Army-type briefing, trying to prepare them for what could be at best, a very demanding trip. At worst, it could be life threatening. We finally began what turned out to be a "character-building" experience for everyone, myself included.

The field trip started by heading south from Jerusalem to

Eilat on the northern edge of the Gulf of Aqaba. There, we rented two elongated, topless jeeps, the kind used in the US Army for small, mobile ambulances, the kind able to carry four patients on litters. I was aware the ability to carry patients might be needed by our green group.

Since our plan called for us to enter into the Sinai desert, the Israeli Army also had some requirements. After almost pleading with us not to go, and finally realizing they could not scare these determined college students out of making this trek, the soldiers gave us a required list of things we had to comply with in order to get the final permission to go.

First, we had to have eight 5-gallon "Jerry cans" of water. Second, we had to have eight 5-gallon cans of gasoline. They reminded us that were no gas stations in the Sinai desert and then, only half-joking, said that unless we could count on getting water out of the rock like Moses did, we would definitely need water. Further, since much of our route was to follow rock-floored wadi (stream) beds, we had to have one spare tire for *each* of the tires on the ground. One clever student turned and counted, as the Army assured us we *would* have flat tires. Little did we know that we would have one flat tire for each of the ten days we were on the trip.

We faced an additional problem of not being able to find any metal 5-gallon cans. We finally located and purchased plastic 5-gallon containers, all brightly colored—red, blue, green and yellow. So with this color caravan of cans, with extra student clothing and with a dozen tires strapped onto the jeeps, we set out for Mount Sinai with our planned course of direction filed with the Israeli Army.

We were truly a sight to behold. In a time of hostilities or war, this carnival-looking caravan would have been a prime target no one could miss. Imagine the Beverly Hillbillies in Jeeps and in Technicolor and you've got it. I could not help but wonder if Moses and the Israelites had looked something like this, only with tens of thousands more people. Even with our small group, we stood out like a multi-colored kaleidoscope moving across the desert floor.

I thought the best position for me was to be in the second jeep. In case anything went wrong, I would be able to see it and signal for a stop. Each jeep had a map. I kept one in the back jeep and I gave the other to a responsible, older student in the lead jeep. Together we went over the entire route we were to take and then I made my first mistake. I gave him the compass to keep us going in the right direction. Even worse, I neglected to tell him one very important point—hold the compass away from the metal dashboard of the jeep.

When we left Eilat that morning we were to go in an easterly direction toward the rising sun in order to get to Mount Sinai. However, by mid-afternoon we were still heading toward the sun. Something was seriously wrong. We were obviously heading west in the afternoon, still looking the sun in the eye, but going in the opposite direction from Mount Sinai. With the compass out of the jeep, I finally determined that we had, in fact, headed toward the rising sun in the east in the morning, but somewhere around noontime in those deceiving desert wadis, we had gotten turned around and were now heading due west. Since the compass was being held on the metal dashboard and magnetized to point straight ahead, my compass man thought we were going in the right direction all along.

Our suspicions were definitely confirmed when we came upon a huge body of water, something obviously not found in the Sinai desert. What we had done was to travel east from Eilat for several miles then somehow we made a slow U-turn. Now after a day's ride, we were right back at the Gulf of Aqaba, about 25-mile south of Eilat. Not a very good first day. Then I recalled that Moses had not even had a compass. Maybe that's the reason it took 40 years.

Actually, the rest of the trip turned out better. There were some personality frictions as you might expect on a trip like that, but it served to round the corners off of some who needed their corners rounded off. Like all days in the Sinai, December days are hot, but the nights were especially windy and bitterly cold. On one occasion, when trying to traverse the side of a hill, one of our jeeps turned over. Amazingly, everybody was able to jump out in time and no one was hurt. With so many shoulders to put to it, we turned the jeep back on all fours and were off again, no worse for the wear, and with a huge tale to tell when we finally got back to the American Institute on Christmas Eve.

Looking back on that year in Jerusalem, the most lasting memory for me at the American Institute was one where Dr. Young spelled out his vision of what the relationship of Christians to Jews could and should look like. It was a vision that I embraced with joy at that time and still do to this day.

The Vision from the Jerusalem Rotary Club

Early in 1970 Dr. Young invited me to attend a Rotary Club meeting that was held weekly at the YMCA in Jerusalem, right across the street from the King David Hotel. The Rotary Club was very special to Dr. Young. He was a past-president of the Jerusalem Rotary and had served on the committee for Rotary International. He very much identified with the Rotary motto: "Service Above Self." As a matter of fact, it was on just that idea Dr. Young was speaking at the meeting for which he had asked me to join him. It had a different twist than I expected. More specifically, he cast a vision of how Christians and Jews might work toward a more harmonious relationship. It was a perfect place for such a talk, because in attendance were Jews and Christians who served in prominent positions throughout Jerusalem.

Basically what Dr. Young envisioned was a new attitude, demonstrated by new behavior on the part of Christians

toward Jews. **His was a call to Christians to show unconditional love to the Jews with no agenda in mind, evan-
gelistic or otherwise.** Dr. Young told the group he would
love to see everybody become Christians, but that showing
support, acceptance, kindness and compassion to Israel and
the Jewish people was the first priority.

He reminded me after the meeting of the Apostle Peter's
admonition, *"Always be prepared to give an answer to
everyone **who asks you** to give the reason for the hope that
you. But do this with gentleness and respect"* (I Peter 3:15).
He said, "Now the responsibilities of Christians are to bless
and love the Jewish people, to build bridges of friendship
through acts of caring and concern, and to follow the
Apostle Paul's admonition to Christians that the Jews are
'now to receive mercy as a result of God's mercy to you'
(Romans 11:30-31)." Also, he stressed that this mercy is to
have a tangible expression, as Paul reminds us, *"For if the
Gentiles have shared in the Jews spiritual blessings, they
owe it to the Jews to **share** with them their material blessings"* (Romans 15:27).

Dr. Young's vision included a mandate to fervently pray
for the peace of Jerusalem and to make every effort to stand
with the Jewish people in practical ways: financially,
morally and spiritually. He deeply felt that a love for Israel
and the Jewish people should visibly unite all Christians,
especially those who firmly believe the Word of God, and
those who are one in the Holy Spirit and *"long for the
Lord's appearing"* (II Timothy 4:8). That was the only time
I attended a Rotary meeting in Jerusalem, so I don't know if
it was their practice to give standing ovations to their speak-
ers, but they certainly did so on that day for Dr. G. Douglas
Young.

Since then, that vision has traveled far and wide. In
1978, Dr. and Mrs. Young retired from the American
Institute to live in Motza Elite in the hills surrounding

Jerusalem. There he continued to work in the organization he founded to carry out his vision, *Bridges for Peace.* Today this organization continues under the able leadership of Clarence H. Wagner, with branches throughout the world, including the USA. After a life of service and teaching, Dr. Young died unexpectedly of a heart attack in 1980. He was buried in the Bishop Gobat cemetery right next to the American Institute grounds that overlook the Judean Hills he loved so much.

Our year came and went so very quickly at the American Institute. Though we wanted to stay and Dr. Young wanted us to stay, the financial situation at the Institute would not allow it. So, just a year later we were going to move our family again. However, this time it was not to an unknown destination, but was back to very familiar turf.

Just before I got out of the Army and before coming to the American Institute, I had received a telephone call from Dr. Hudson Armerding, President of Wheaton College. He had heard that I was getting out of the Army and asked me to consider coming to Wheaton as the Chaplain. I had told him what a great honor it was to be considered for such a post at Wheaton but that I was committed to at least one year in Israel. "Let's do this, Jim," he said, "You go ahead and see how it works out in Israel. I'll keep the position open for a year and then we'll see what the Lord does." I thanked him for this generous offer and agreed to be in prayer about it during the coming year.

When I knew that we were not going to able to stay at the Institute more than one year, I wrote to Dr. Armerding. His return letter assured me that the position was mine and that he was looking forward to our coming to Wheaton as Chaplain to students, staff and faculty. Imagine the great blessing this was to my family to know we were going to Wheaton. Not only did we not have to wait and wonder about future ministry, but we were being so enthusiastically welcomed. Even on the airplane going home, Patty began to prepare the children for our new life by teaching them to sing our alma mater's song, "Wheaton, dear ole Wheaton, live forever, Brave sons and daughters true."

As we flew out of Israel and watched the Land vanish from sight, I asked myself, "Is this the end of Israel for us?" Surely not. I could see no foreseeable niche for us in Israel. To leave Israel was like leaving home as we left friends we had bonded with forever. We parted with deep, loving relationships that have lasted a lifetime. I sensed in my heart of hearts that somehow, someway, in His time, God would bring us back, but I had no idea how or when that would happen. Before we go forward, Patty will share her memories of our getting out of the Army and our first trip to Israel.

Patty's Perspective

The Promised Land

The Army packed our belongings and we sent them for storage, then we prepared to get on the plane and fly to Israel. Before we drove off the post at Ft. Devens, I went one last time to see my good friend, Libby Greene, the wife of our commanding officer, Colonel Vernon Greene. We cried some more, hugged and then pulled away for a last goodbye.

Her last words to me were said jokingly, "Don't go over there and become a Jew." We both just laughed and I drove away.

It is probably impossible for a Bible-believing Christian to go to Israel and not be moved. I had been aware as long as I could remember of Jerusalem, Bethlehem, the Jordan River, the Hill of Golgotha, the Garden Tomb, and the Galilee. I knew as much about the names of Israel as I did of the towns in Louisiana—and Jesus was as He always had been - the core or my life, the very purpose of living. I was taught to live always with the expectation of the return of Jesus, when "His feet will stand on the Mount of Olives."

So to fly into Israel was an experience that can only be described as awesome, like that of a little child trembling with excitement the first time he sees a lighted Christmas tree. It reminds me of the time when I took T.J. and Nathan, two of our oldest grandchildren, to the beach. All the way over I kept saying, "The beach is *SO BIG*," and Nathan kept saying "Granny, it can't be that big."

Each time we passed either the Chesapeake or some smaller body of water, he asked, "Is this the beach, Granny?"

"No, Nathan, it is *much bigger* than this."

Finally, as we approached the ocean but before we could see the beach, I told them, "We're almost there. We're almost there. Wait until you see it, it is *SO BIG*."

As we drove very slowly over the last hill in Virginia Beach and the car leveled off so we could finally see, I looked back at the boys. Nathan's mouth had dropped open and his huge eyes were scanning the horizon in disbelief while his body trembled with awe at his first sight of the Atlantic Ocean. That's what it was like to fly in over the Mediterranean and approach Israel for first time.

Even driving from the Lod Airport through hot, dusty, ochre landscapes seemed out of the ordinary, but to start up that winding road to Jerusalem, the city that has captivated the imaginations of the nations for centuries, was truly breathtaking. From there on it was one day after another seeing all the places we had only dreamed of and read about.

Although I had not found college French classes to be motivating, I was downright fascinated with Hebrew and took to it immediately with a passion. Whether we went to the Mount of Olives, to Golgotha, to the Garden Tomb, I strained to try to read the signs as soon as I knew the alphabet. We walked in and out of every gate of Jerusalem, up and down the streets of the Via Dolorosa, through every Quarter in Jerusalem, trying to cover every inch possible. We prayed at the Wailing Wall and put little written prayer requests in the cracks of the rocks.

The day we got on a boat and went across the Galilee there was actually a storm. We remembered Jesus walking on these waters and calming a storm. We went to Bethlehem and saw where Jesus was born and to the place where David picked up the stone that slew Goliath. All of our children were baptized again in the Jordan River and we climbed every mountain and hill in Israel. Within a short period of time, we breathed and lived and walked our way through almost every place mentioned in the entire Bible and every time we went anywhere, Jim got out the Bible and read a portion related to that particular place.

All the people of the Land were incredible, and even an old woman in the Old City of Jerusalem sitting on the street holding a pan of grapes seemed like someone we knew or wanted to know. Jews and Arabs alike were friendly and hospitable. Our babysitter Henriette was a beautiful Arab Christian teenager who not only spoke perfect English, but also perfect Hebrew, Arabic, and French.

We became close friends with Sarah and Shimon, an orthodox Jewish couple whose parents had crawled over the border from Russia to come to Israel. They bought separate dishes so that they could have us eat in their totally orthodox home. We purchased dishes, utensils and cups just for their use. I washed them without letting them touch anything, and stored them so that they were kosher for eating cake and drinking coffee at our home. The cake was easy. We just bought one at the local market and used the koshered knife to cut it. We met Russians who had never seen a Bible, and we went to homes of Arab friends in Bethlehem to eat meals with them.

For Sunday worship we attended many churches, but

settled in at a Baptist church in Jerusalem on Narkis Street, pastored by Dr. Bob Lindsey, a brilliant scholar and author from Oklahoma who came to Israel before 1948. In addition to his duties at the American Institute, Jim also served as interim pastor at this Baptist church when Dr. Lindsey was on a short sabbatical back in the USA. Today that church is called the Jerusalem Congregation and is pastored by good friends, Charles and Liz Kopp.

Our home was bare, but homey, and we settled into our new life with a minimum of adjustments. Everything was fascinating and new, and we thought it would never end.

It wasn't the fact that we didn't have much money and I had begun to adjust somewhat to leaving the Army, but I think the rats were the first thing that began to change me and chip away at my heart. Rats were in the house and they were huge. In fact, we could not eat food that was left out, nor could we store anything on shelves without seeing little droppings shortly afterwards. My solution was to put all the dishes, glasses and eating utensils in the refrigerator and go to the store every single day for fresh foods. Since small stores, or mekolets, are on almost every corner, that part was not hard to do.

However, one night when I was fast asleep, I felt something move on the bed and reached out my hand to feel a large rat running over my body. I had been raised in the country in our small town of Winnfield, Lousiana, so I knew about rats, roaches, snakes, mosquitoes and most creeping, crawling creatures. We didn't have air conditioning and usually left our windows open and our doors unlocked, but I never worried about anything or anyone coming into our house. Certainly, if any creepy, crawling creature dared to enter our house, my Daddy knew what to do to mercilessly extinguish them all.

This rat problem in Jerusalem may sound wimpish for people who have braved the trials of the world, but things began to change for me. I worried mostly for our children, and prayers became very simple, "Lord, keep the rats from biting the children." I found enough empty, large coffee cans to put under the four feet of each of our beds. Then I filled them about two-thirds with water so that, hopefully, rats would fall in and drown. We bought these gigantic Israeli mousetraps, really rat-traps, and cheesed them up each night before going to bed. Somehow were able to contain this problem.

Winter came and it was very cold, worsened by damp stone walls and our having only one small coal-oil heater in the middle of the living room. It gave new meaning to "central heating." Every day we had to buy a can of heating oil and pour it in the small opening in the back of the heater, without spilling it on the stove and blowing up the house. I had known about kerosene heaters, but this was an old, old dangerous stove. I kept reminding myself that this house was in one of the good sections of town.

When a friend came to our home for a meal one night and sat in one of our old chairs, he fell straight through it. But then another friend brought us a better one the next day. We purchased some secondhand lawn furniture from who-knows-where and draped it with blankets Henriette bargained for in the Old City. I cut up white muslin sheets to make curtains with my little Featherweight Singer Sewing Machine, which I had fortunately had the good sense to bring with us. With some fast art on white butcher paper, strengthened to hang on the wall by gluing dowels on the top and bottom, we covered the walls with drawings and letters of the alphabet.

We quickly learned never to leave anything on the porch or in the yard at night. Any and all items simply vanished by morning. The locals told of people grabbing the watch off of anyone who stuck out his hand to signal a turn when driving through town. However, in those years, it was basically safe to go anywhere and talk to anyone in Israel, a far cry from the sad, vanished state of peace today.

Somewhere along about that time I began to sleep less and worry more. I did have devotions, memorized Scriptures, prayed and continued with life, but things began to feel tighter and tighter around me. One day when I was driving down the highway listening to an English radio station, I heard an announcement that Elvis Presley had died. I began to literally sob. It didn't take a psychiatrist to know that something was wrong. I never listened to Elvis Presley that much and though I didn't have anything against him, I knew that Elvis Presley was not my problem.

On another day, I was driving along a highway and began to think of the possibility of being buried in a graveyard that was not near my Daddy. This time I pulled over on the side of the road and cried for several minutes. A policeman came up behind me, got out of the car and asked me if I was all right. I told him, still sobbing, that I didn't want to be buried in a country where my Daddy was not.

He responded very gently, "Oh, I'm so sorry that your father passed away."

I got control of myself, looked at him and said, "My Daddy didn't die. I just don't want to be buried in a country where he doesn't live."

He looked very compassionately at me and suggested that I go on home, which I did.

Rachel—Near Death...Healed by God

Then Rachel got sick. We had just celebrated her first birthday with a party a week or two before. Now all of a sudden she began to look pale. At first it seemed like a cold or some simple thing, but in a day or two she had high fever and had to have aspirin every three to four hours to keep it controlled. This went on for days while we took her first to a local doctor, then to Hadassah Hospital. No one was able to come up with an adequate diagnosis and she continued to decline.

Finally, she just lay in her bed most of the time, not able to sit up, not able to crawl anymore. We were losing her and there didn't seem to be anything anyone could do about it. By now I was seriously beginning to wonder what in the world we were doing here. Where this all would end? I longed for the Army and I had never been that scared.

Trips to Bible places were over. Now we just hunkered down to prayer and reading God's Word. Nothing else mattered to me if my beloved babies were not doing well. Even my efforts to appear cheerful were futile and I was struggling with deep depression and fear. Jim talked to Bob Lindsey about my condition, and Bob said that I was suffering partly from culture shock. He further told him that some people never get over culture shock. When Jim told me what he said, for the first time in my life I realized that I was in over my head and that I might be like this forever. That was one of the most frightening experiences of my entire life and I began to seriously cry out to the Lord for help.

We were alone one evening when someone knocked on the door. Jim went to open it and there stood Charles Kopp, his wife Liz, and his father, Mr. Kopp. As Mr. Kopp began to enter the room, he abruptly stopped, looked around and said with the assurance of Elijah, "Satan is trying to kill someone in this house." To say that we welcomed him into the house is an understatement. We told him about Rachel. We went into the living room, where he related to us how God was working in various places he had just been. He talked about faith and healing, and although we did not go into the baby's room that night, he did pray before he left. Somehow that evening a wee bit of burden began to lift.

The very next day we were with several people who had come to Israel for a conference. As we sat around the room, people began to speak of the power of God, of miracles, of faith and of being filled with the Holy Spirit. I remember trying to edge myself into the conversation and ask some questions. Each time, someone would quickly turn to me and give me a short answer, as though they just assumed that I knew all there was to know and didn't need any attention.

With a sick child on my mind and not to be denied, I continued to try to get answers and finally one person turned to me and handed me a small booklet entitled, "How to be Filled with the Holy Spirit." I had studied about the Holy Spirit for years in church and college. During seminary years, I read everything Jim read. I had plowed my way through every word of thick, academic books written about every biblical aspect of the Holy Spirit known to man. I mean this was serious, seminary stuff.

I knew that it is impossible to say that Jesus is Lord without the Holy Spirit being in your life. I knew that God worked by the Holy Spirit and I could quote dozens of verses about the ministry of the Holy Spirit. I knew that one should not quench the Holy Spirit by any sins, acts or thoughts that are displeasing to God or against His written word. But I had never, ever heard of praying to be filled with the Holy Spirit as these people were speaking of. I was definitely interested and knew I needed whatever God had to offer.

So I scanned the book quickly, and nudged into the conversation to ask another question. I got little response, but across the room I could not help but notice Charles Kopp watching this entire scenario. He was only nineteen and had not been brought into the conversation in any significant way that evening. In fact, I don't recall that he said a word that evening, but after the meeting he came over to me and said that he would love to come to our home and talk about being filled with the Holy Spirit. I quickly agreed and he came the very next day. By that time I had read and reread the booklet and was ready for whatever he had to offer.

In short, that evening Charles prayed over me for almost two hours, crying out to the Lord, speaking in tongues, patiently working over me like a loving doctor hovers over a sick patient. As he prayed and spoke Scriptures, I began to grow in my spirit to believe God. He rebuked spirits of unbelief like the Apostle Paul would have done and covered every possible impediment known to man to my being filled with the Holy Spirit. Although he observed me, he never pressed me to speak in tongues and I did not at that time. But when the prayers were over, I knew beyond a shadow of a doubt that I was filled with the Holy Spirit.

There have been several watershed experiences in my life, like the time I went forward in a meeting and personally gave my life to Jesus Christ as my Savior. Life was never the same after that. Not everything changed, but some things changed forever. That was the way it was that night when Charles Kopp prayed over me. Since that time, I have experienced God in a deeper, more trusting way. Before, I had believed in Jesus for salvation and believed in the Bible in general, but had not believed much that was in the Bible. I had prayed for twenty years for my brother to quit drinking, but it never really occurred to me that he might. I quoted verses about not being afraid, but continued to almost invite fear. I could believe for eternal issues, but not for day-to-day living.

One of the most obvious and exciting results of being filled with the Holy Spirit was that basic, underlying, and in some cases unknown fears I had from childhood literally vanished that night. I never again got up several times in the night to see if my children were still breathing. When Jim went out the door in the morning, I did not envision his not coming back. Fear of diseases and anticipation of doom left me. Just as I had known forever after I came to Jesus that I was saved and would spend eternity in heaven, so after this evening I knew that God was empowering me to believe

Him for other things.

The next morning, Jim suggested that we anoint Rachel with oil according to James 5 and pray to God for her healing. For the first time in my life I really believed and knew in advance that this was definitely going to happen. We put our little worn-out baby on the bed and gathered the children around her to pray. Jim got some olive oil from Bethlehem out of the kitchen and as he came back with oil from that Holy Place, my heart jumped in faith. I knew this baby was going to live, not die.

Each one of us, Matt and Sarah included, poured a little oil on our fingers and placed our fingers on her sweet, suffering little body and cried out to our God. Within an hour she began to perk up and by evening she was sitting up and crawling again. Nothing but the power of the Holy Spirit of our Awesome God could accomplish that miracle, and this great gift of mercy and grace changed our lives forever. In the very land where our Lord Jesus had lived and healed others, we had personally found that He lives and heals today. Israel forever took on new meaning for me after that precious day in Jerusalem when God stooped down to heal our sweet Rachel.

CHAPTER 6

Back to Orange and Blue: Chaplain at Wheaton College

Returning to Wheaton was like coming home. For me, Wheaton was my first spiritual home after coming to faith in Jesus. The home of the Orange and the Blue was where, as a student, my faith as a new Christian had been nurtured. Here I experienced the mentoring care of faculty, coaches and fellow students. Here I grew and matured as a young man having found God, and it was here my love for Israel was reinforced and began to take shape. It was at my alma mater that I received a call to the ministry that initially led me into the Army Chaplaincy. Central to my entire future, it was here that I met Patty. "Wheaton, dear Ole Wheaton, live forever," is the school song. Since Wheaton is where God sent Patty to me, I will be eternally grateful for this gracious gift.

Dr. Hudson Armerding was president of Wheaton at that time and was the one who had recruited me to be Wheaton's new chaplain. He had served in the Navy during World War II and had retired as Commander in the Naval Reserves. He felt that Wheaton needed a military chaplain. This was a bit surprising since there was a lot of anti-Vietnam sentiment on the college campuses of the country at that time.

While anti-Vietnam sentiment was a little late in getting to Wheaton, it was there nevertheless. I found, however, once I got to be known and once I got to know some of the students, my military background was no hindrance to the ministry. In fact I found it to be an asset. Many of the students, as well as the faculty, were interested in knowing how an Airborne Ranger, Special Forces, Vietnam veteran, combat chaplain had found his way to Wheaton College. I must confess it was a major cultural adjustment for me—one I didn't fully make until years later. There was a restlessness and unsettledness I had coming out of Vietnam that took some time to resolve. The year spent in Israel only served to prolong the adjustment since it represented a new emotional high in itself.

Initially, the greatest challenge in coming to Wheaton as the chaplain was that I was following in the footsteps of a virtual icon. Dr. Evan Welsh, who was a spiritual institution, had been the beloved chaplain of the Wheaton family for years. He had been our chaplain when Patty and I were students. We had loved him like a spiritual father. I found out early on in the Wheaton experience that one does not replace or duplicate the ministry of a revered saint of God. One simply attempts to establish his own identity and allow time for God to confirm the ministry.

Dr. Armerding was a great help and encouragement in that transition. He had assumed the Presidency of Wheaton while another highly revered and former Wheaton President, Dr. V. Raymond Edmond, was serving as Chancellor of the College. Dr. Armerding had to make a similar transitional adjustment and advised me to be patient and in due time my own bona fides as chaplain would be established. It was good advice and came about just as he predicted.

No sooner had we settled into the fall semester than a series of messages began to be passed on to me regarding a mission conference to be held on the campus of the University of Illinois at Urbana. It was being sponsored by Inter Varsity and was to take place the week between

Christmas and New Year's, and its focus was on challenging college age people to consider God's call to the mission field. I had heard of this conference before when I was a student at Wheaton, but had never attended. Inter Varsity hosted this conference every four years, and 1970 was to be the year for the next Urbana Conference.

I saw this as an opportunity to get a number of Wheaton students to think seriously about serving the Lord on the mission field. Little did I know, at the time, of the significant impact it would have on me, my family and the future of our ministry. Let me set the historical context.

The Relationship between Jews and Christians

During our time in Israel, I made a number of observations regarding the relationship of Jews and Israelis to gentiles and Christians. One observation was that these two seemed to be polarized—a kind of "us and them" mentality existed. One of the questions I pondered when we had gone to Israel was "Who really is Israel?" Having graduated from Dallas Theological Seminary, and having high esteem for the faculty there, I was naturally predisposed to the major tenant of Dispensational Theology: namely, the distinction between the Church and Israel.

However, as I studied the Scriptures regarding this issue once we had arrived in Israel, I became convinced that in some very important sense, Israel and the church were one. It wasn't until years later that I fully understood the significance of that initial insight. Others had made that connection, some for good and others with disastrous results.

Indeed, many through the ages who said the Church has superceded Israel (commonly referred to as Replacement Theology, or Supersessionism) had sown the seeds of Christian anti-Semitism, in some cases bearing horrific fruit in such evils as occurred during the Crusades, the Inquisition and the mother of all horrors, the Holocaust. If heresy can be defined as, "a deliberate denial of revealed truth coupled with the acceptance of error," (*Evangelical Dictionary of Theology*, pp. 508), then Replacement Theology could be considered as heresy.

I could see from the Scripture that the early Church in Jerusalem was distinctively Jewish in the expression of its faith. Even after the conversion of Cornelius in Acts 10, and also in the writing of the letters and the epistles, the religious and spiritual context into which the writers were speaking was obviously Jewish. Gentile converts were being discipled within the framework of biblical Judaism (cf. Acts 15:21).

What occurred to me then was the need to recapture the setting and the experience of the believing community of the first century. This would be a setting where the differences between Jewish and gentile followers of the Messiah Jesus were minimal and the practicing faith of the people of God would be a mirror image of what was then a growing sect within Judaism, namely the Nazarene Sect (Acts 24:25).

Institutional and denominational Christianity, as well as the established Church, did not come into being until at least the 4th century. Christianity was an unknown term to the first readers of the New Testament and the word "Christian" is found only three times, in Acts 11:26, 26:28 and I Peter 4:16. In none of these instances is it a term that followers of the Messiah Jesus used to describe themselves.

So, exactly what was their religious faith and what did they call themselves? The answer is, their religion was a form of Judaism that included the "Nazarene Sect" just as it did the sects of the Pharisees and Sadducees. They called themselves the followers of "The Way" (Acts 19:9, 23; 22:4; 24:14, 22).

Still, the question that was constantly gnawing at me was, "Why couldn't we reproduce or replicate that today?" It would certainly make it a lot easier for Jews who wanted to become followers of Jesus, especially if they knew they were not leaving biblical Judaism. Plus it would put gentile believers in Jesus back in touch with their spiritual roots and give added understanding of their rightful religious heritage—a heritage that has been sundered from its original source and all but lost in what we know as institutional Christianity.

It is perhaps unrealistic to think that after 2000 years, the institutional structure of Christianity could be revamped. It is deeply entrenched in the lives of most Christians. But isn't there something we could do to recover the roots of our faith? Are we to be forever detached from the religious mother that birthed us?

I was not prepared for the possible answers and challenges the conference at Urbana 70 was going to present. Now, coming back to Wheaton and having this opportunity to take a group of students to what would be a life-determining experience, was indeed a privilege. I'm not sure how many students' lives were changed, but I know for certain that my life's direction was changed forever.

The Impact of Dr. Donald A. McGavran

As Providence would have it, I saw on the schedule a workshop entitled "Communicating the Gospel Cross Culturally." My interest was piqued since I was looking for ways and means to somehow relate cross culturally to Israel and the Jewish people. Unknown to me, the workshop was being taught by a legend in missiology, Dr. Donald A. McGavran.

After over thirty years on the mission field in India, Dr. McGavran had published a book entitled *The Bridges of God: A Study in the Strategy of Missions.* This book literally rocked the world of missions thinking and has been a primary change agent since it was published in 1955.

Among the many classic statements Dr. McGavran is noted for is, "Men like to become Christians without crossing racial, linguistic and class barriers." (McGavren, 1970, page 198) McGavren was all about removing barriers that hindered people from coming to faith. One of his most compelling examples of barriers comes from the early church.

"During the first fifteen years of the Church's history, almost *all* believers became Christians *while remaining members of the Jewish community.* ...

Nineteen hundred hears ago the Church found that the Jews liked to become Christians without crossing racial barriers. The Jewish caste was a tightly knit society, it had effective control, it insisted that Jews marry Jews. It ostracized women who "went wrong" with men of other races. ... The Jewish cast had no dealings with the half-breed Samaritans. In foreign cities, Jews lived in their own wards. Distant Jews sometimes married back onto Jerusalem families, as in the case of Paul's sister. ... As long as Jews could become Christians within Judaism, the Church could and did grow amazingly among Jews, filling Jerusalem, Judea and Galilee. ... When the Church began to grow in the synagogue communities around the Mediterranean, the first to become disciples of Christ were devout Jews who had been eagerly expecting the Messiah. Those becoming Christians within the synagogue could do so without crossing racial and class barriers." (McGavren, 1970, pages 201-202)

As I look back, I can say without doubt, Urbana 1970 was a turning point in my thinking and Dr. Donald McGavren was the man who made it happen. I would only add that Church, or "congregations" should be with a little "c," in order to better grasp the understanding of the Jewish context of those first centuries of followers of Jesus. And the word Christ should be understood not as the last name of Jesus, but as the Greek word for the Hebrew word for Messiah. I could see for the first time that the relationship between Jews and Christians had to be considered in the context of the Judaism of the first century. I saw that Jews at that time who were accepting Jesus as the long-promised Messiah of Israel were doing so as Jews, within the context of their own culture of Judaism. They were not denying the faith of their fathers nor their ethnicity as Jews. This was no great theological leap nor was it a huge cultural stretch.

Not all first century Jews accepted Jesus, as we know, but practically all who did accept Jesus in the first century(s) were Jews. They simply believed like the Apostle Paul when he confessed before Felix, *"I admit that I worship the God of our fathers, as a follower of the Way, which they call a sect. I believe everything that agrees with the Law and that is written in the Prophets"* (Acts 24:14).

The whole Urbana 70 experience begged the question, "Why couldn't this happen again?" Why couldn't a distinctively Jewish context exist that would encourage Jews to view Jesus from the perspective of first century Judaism? It was successful then; why not now? However, in my enthusiasm and excitement over this newfound insight, little did I realize the indelible impact of two thousand years of horrific Christian anti-Semitism, which would dictate against such an option for most Jews, but more on that later.

Going back to Wheaton from Urbana, my mind was a whirl. Among the thoughts that began to emerge was the question, "How could this be demonstrated to the Jewish community?" How could it be shown today that a Jew who follows Jesus is not an anomaly and that a Jew who believes in Jesus is not a contradiction in terms? Certainly there had been Jews who have become Christians throughout the centuries. Most churches today have Jewish converts within their congregations, but for all practical purposes, these Jews have lost their ties with their ethnic and theological heritage. For some Jews this is OK. But for most it is not. Most will not make such a demanding and self-denying leap. Nor should they, I would add.

My mind was in a whirl, returning to Wheaton from Urbana. A different dimension to this issue began to surface. I began to realize that if this alternative for Jews was ever going to be a viable option, it would have to be visibly demonstrated. At that point, Paul's profound insight came to mind, *"To the Jews I became like a Jew, to win the Jews"* (I Corinthians 9:20). The obvious question is, "How do you become a Jew to a Jew?" What does that mean? Can a Christian do that? Can a non-Jew do that? Should a non-Jew do that?

We had heard of other non-Jewish followers of Jesus who had attempted to identify with Jews, but the effort had been fraught with problems. Still the question lingered, "How does one become a Jew to Jews?" These were the thoughts and questions I brought home to Patty from the Urbana experience, thoughts we began to process together.

Our interests in becoming a Jew were about to blossom and take a new turn.

Patty's Perspective

Someone said you can't go back home, but I figured that they didn't know about Wheaton. I had known I was going to Wheaton College as long as I knew I was going to college at all. My 15-year-older sister, Wanda Ann Mercer, had told me so. When I was only four years old, Sister, as I called her, had left home to go to work, first to Washington, D.C. and later to Wheaton to work with Young Life, a high school program started by Jim Rayburn to reach unchurched kids.

I literally lived much of the year waiting for her annual Christmas visit back to Winnfield, Louisiana. As she opened up my sights to far away places, Daddy was working on keeping me close to home. While he kept promising to buy me a car if I would stay and go to college in Louisiana, Mama was reading the materials and catalog from the Registrar's Office and looking at maps of Chicago. My sweet Irish Daddy never had a chance. I graduated from high school one warm, humid evening in May and boarded the train for Chicago early the next morning, with a scruffy suitcase full of secondhand clothes, a shoebox full of Daddy's chicken and a young heart bursting with both fear and fascination.

I had always thought that I would major in math since I had taken every course offered in high school and done well. To me, solid geometry and trigonometry were fun, not work. I did anything with numbers in it for fun. But when I told my high school mentor near the end of senior year that I planned to major in math in college, I was shocked when he emphatically said, "No, Patty, do **not** major in math." Putting aside the question as to why he had not mentioned this four years earlier, I asked "Why?" He told me that women could not get jobs in math. In this day of equal rights for women, it's hard to imagine such things being said, but this was in the deep South before integration, much less women's rights. Having been taught to honor my elders and not really given to rebellion anyway, I said "Okay," and decided to think about it later.

The first years in college I mostly took the courses Sister told me to take. I had thought about being a teacher. Since I had played a pretty good game of basketball in high school, I thought I'd like to teach and coach girl's basketball. She nixed that and also told me not to major in education, sociology, missions or physical education. And she said, "Forget Latin." I suggested Spanish and she said, "No, take French." Somewhat frustrated, I systematically began to sign up for general requirements for graduation and put off as long as possible what I would major in. Since I had to work all summer, most holidays and over 20 hours a week to pay my way through college, I knew options were limited. In returning to classes my junior year, I was no closer to a major than when first enrolled. Finally I got the catalog, a pen and paper, and approached it like a math problem.

After crossing off every major I had no interest in or that required taking other prerequisites, I settled on two courses of study that could be completed in two years: art and psychology. After a day or so of not being able to decide between these two strangers, I did a very biblical thing by following the example of the High Priest of Israel who used the Urim and Thummin for seeking God's will in making decisions. Well, at least somewhat like it. Since no one knew exactly what the Urim and Thummin were, I flipped a coin. I like to say, "Art thinks it won."

Without ever having taken instruction of any kind in art, I began in earnest to learn to paint and draw, and to study art history. After studying in many colleges and art schools, earning an M.F.A. in Art Theory and Practice at Northwestern University in Evanston, Illinois, and teaching at the Corcoran College of Art and Design in Washington, D.C., it is possible to report that I never looked back to question that coin toss.

Now with a husband and three children, I was coming back to my alma mater. Again, I was a happy camper. Not only did I like a college town in general, but I liked Wheaton. We talked with a good friend who was the Dean, Dr. Richard Gross, about what salary we should expect. We will never forget his good advice, "They are going to suggest 'Nine Thousand,' and you are going to say, 'Thirteen.'"

That doesn't sound like much today, but it was part of a package that included living in the Chaplain's manse, right next door to a campus dorm. So we moved in with what furniture we had and in no time, the small, white, wooden house, under the shadow of a huge men's dorm, was ready for company. And company we had, day and night. As a young mother with three small children and a dog, college kids were actually welcomed. There were limitless names to call for any babysitting need, and at least weekly someone would help find and retrieve our dog who had wandered off. Most of the time students were just looking for a home away from home and glad to be in any house.

We had a standing rule. Everyone was welcome to go in the kitchen and make toast. I bought loaves of day-old bread and giant tubs of margarine. We had another rule, "Never on Sunday." We had just returned from Israel and were quite accustomed to keeping the Sabbath, so we just transferred the rules to Sunday. I made a sign for the door, "Not on Sunday. Come back tomorrow unless it is an emergency. Go home and rest."

While we had lived in Israel, we had come in close contact with dozens of ideas. One of them had been the kosher laws. A Christian family had given us a book to read, entitled *None of These Diseases.* After reading it and thoroughly studying the food laws in the Bible, we determined that we would eat only what the Bible said we could eat. In fact, we had a huge pork loin in the refrigerator at the time, but after considering starting kosher laws a couple of days later, we decided to give it to some friends and start immediately.

So a Louisiana Cajun girl who had grown up out in the country eating "anything that moves," gave up pork, bacon, shrimp, lobster, clams, crabs, jambalaya, and craw fish pie. And when we explained it to the children, Jim slowly read to them from the Bible the list of other things we could not eat: moles, rabbits, squirrels, horses, dogs, cats, lions, camels, eagles, vultures, buzzards, kites, owls, storks, herons, hoopees, snakes, alligators, crocodiles, bears, bats and rats. We didn't make a big deal of it, we just explained that God had given these rules for our best interest, and we wanted to try to follow them. After he finished with the list and asked if there were any questions, Matt said, "Dad, do people really eat kites?"

The children never asked about it again and we proceeded at Wheaton College to apply to our lives the new understanding we believed we received from living in Israel.

Chaplain Hutchens participates with Battalion
Commander Lt. Colonel John Tyler in memorial
service for the men killed on Hill 65.

One-year birthday party for Rachel -
right before she got sick.

Jim baptizing Matt in the Jordan River.

Hutchens family and
Wellington at Fuller Seminary in California

Brigadier General Jim in
Washington, D.C.

Loading Jeeps for Mt.Sinai trip

Hutchens family in Jerusalem

Yaakov in Ramat Hasharon, Israel

Sarah in movie in Israel - The Phantom Kid

Ft. Bragg, North Carolina - 6th Special Forces luncheon

Graduation day for Matt at West Point Military Academy

"Will they tegaresh" Yael?"

Matt, the actor and Patty and kids
in Ramat Hasharon

Chaplain Hutchens conducting
riverside service in Vietnam

Matt, the Banker, in movie, The Phantom Kid

Rachel back in Virginia

Sarah back in Virginia

American Institute students and Jim on top of Mt. Sinai

Pastor Charles and Liz Kopp and Mr. Kopp

Rachel with a friend Rachel in Ramat Hasharon

The family today in Virginia

Yael (Patty) at **Eli's house** in Ramat Hasharon

CHAPTER 7

"To the Jews I became a Jew" – Almost Accepted

Upon our return to Wheaton, Patty resumed her art studies. She had graduated from Wheaton with a BA in Art, and in the year I spent in Vietnam, she and the children had returned to Wheaton, where she taught in the art department. Now that we were back in the Wheaton/Chicago area, she began to pursue a graduate degree at the Art Institute of Chicago.

During lunch breaks, she would occasionally visit a nearby synagogue for a noontime lecture and just to try to keep up with Hebrew language in a non-Hebrew world. On one occasion, she noticed on a bulletin board a notice of instructions for those considering conversion to Judaism. It gave the time, place, content and duration of the instruction. Almost casually, she inquired about the classes with one of the rabbis and was told of an orientation class designed for those considering conversion. That evening when she came home, almost in passing, she told me about the bulletin board incident.

With our interest in Israel and the Jewish people, plus the recent Urbana experience, this notice began to strike a chord in my thinking. I wondered if we should we look into this. Is this a sign from God? What about Jesus in all this? Is this a natural way we could become a Jew to the Jews today?

Remember, I am the Chaplain of Wheaton College, one of the premier Christian colleges in America. Now I was discussing with my wife the possibility of converting to Judaism. This is not normal. This is not acceptable. This is not only thinking outside the box; it's thinking outside the planet. Does this make good sense? We love Jesus, and we love his people. But we love Israel and the Jewish people. Must these two affections be forever polarized? Must we be satisfied to be schizophrenic in our commitments? Is there no way to bring Jesus and the Jews, the two loves of our lives, together?

Our decision, after much prayer and discussion of the possible implications, was to attend the orientation class and to pursue the conversion process as far as we could. Patty and I agreed that we would not and could not finalize the conversion process without retaining our belief in Jesus. Obviously we were Christians who were considering conversion to Judaism, but in our case we would be keeping Jesus. Would that be possible in Judaism today? Would it even be acceptable?

Of course, we knew it was in the first century and we were convinced it should be an option today. We had no idea if it was possible or not, but we thought the conversion classes would at least end up being an in-depth, intellectually stimulating exposure to the heart and basics of Judaism. Indeed, they were that . . . and more.

The classes were a wonderful learning experience. We learned the background and relevance of all the feasts and festivals of Judaism. As we took the classes each week, we poured over the Bible at home and became absorbed with learning how much of our own faith, as well as the Christian calendar, was inseparably linked to these God-ordained holy days. Passover is the background for the Lord's Supper. The Last Supper was a Passover meal. Pentecost is built on Shavuot, the feast of weeks. Yom Kippur, the Day of Atonement which required a perfect lamb to be sacrificed for sin, prefigures the redeeming, atoning sacrifice of Jesus for the sins of the world.

We learned that the holiest day of all was the Sabbath, and what a joyous delight it is to those who see it as God's gift to mankind. We personally realized how the official pronouncements of a powerful institution unnecessarily antagonized the Jews when they proclaimed Sunday the Lord's day and demanded it replace the Bible's Sabbath. In classes, we learned of the central importance of the Torah, the first five books of the Hebrew Scriptures (the Old Testament), sometimes used to refer to the teaching of all the Old Testament.

We personally became convinced that many of the presumed conflicts of Old Testament with New Testament, between Judaism and Christianity, were self-imposed and in many cases nonexistent. Once again, we were convinced that if somehow the context of the first century could be recaptured and fleshed out, much of what polarizes Judaism and Christianity today might vanish.

Each one of the classes served not only to enrich our own understanding of our faith but to motivate us to learn more. The issue of renouncing Jesus never came up. In fact, the issue of the Messiah never came up.

We were instructed that the last day of the process was to include three things. My son and I would go through a token form of circumcision. Since both of us were already circumcised, it would only be necessary for the Mohel (the man who performs the circumcision) to draw sufficient blood to stain a piece of cotton.

Though Matt was only ten years old he seemed to really understand the significance of our desire to identify with the Jewish people. After living in Israel, he knew what was necessary for that. As I look back, I know he was a real trooper in allowing his blood to be drawn. He has always been one of my heroes for his great sensitivity to spiritual matters and for his deep faithfulness and commitment to his family.

Also, all the members of the family were required to go unclothed into a Mikvah (baptismal tank), dip into the waters three times and respond affirmatively to questions the Rabbi would present at that time. Matt and I went into separate facilities from Patty and the girls.

With the girls, an Orthodox Jewish woman oversaw all the preparations. First, they showered, washed their hair, clipped their fingernails and were checked to make sure they were properly cleansed and everything was kosher. Further, women may not enter the Mikveh during the period of menses. Finally, after a clean sheet was placed on one side for privacy, when everything was prepared and in order and when Patty was in the Mikveh with the girls, three rabbis came into the room to observe the baptism. First, the girls were dipped with Patty assisting. Sarah could immerse herself but Rachel was too young to do it without her mother's help. After immersion, the girls were wrapped in a towel and taken by the orthodox women to dress. Then Patty immersed herself three times. Questions were with each immersion in the waters. (No doubt this is exactly what John the Baptizer did with thousands who immersed themselves in the Jordan River). Here are some of the questions:

"Will you endeavor the keep the Sabbath to best of your ability?"

"Will you keep and honor the feasts and festivals of Judaism?"

"Will you strive to live by the teaching of the Torah?"

For all of us, after "Yes" to each question, we then immersed ourselves completely, making sure the water covered our bodies entirely.

The third part of the conversion procedure was for Patty and me to be officially married by the rabbi under a Chuppah, with the traditional smashing of a glass and drinking a sip of wine. Finally, we would be given Jewish names. The process came to a halt; however, after Matt and I had finished going through the Mikvah (baptism) and the girls were still in the Mikveh.

After Matt and I dried off and dressed, the rabbi brought a document for me to sign. He said our signatures were required to finalize the conversion process. Everything was acceptable until we came to a requirement which read, **"I renounce all former faiths with their messianic and theological tenants."** After seeing that I was unwilling to sign, the rabbi went in to Patty who was still in the Mikvah and asked her, "Do you believe Jesus is the Messiah, too?"

"Yes, I do," she said, but added, "Rabbi, you never said anything about the Messiah in the lessons." Now we were at an impasse. We had met all the requirements up to that point, but obviously would not renounce Jesus, who had actually been the *reason* we had turned to Judaism in the first place. We told the rabbi it was our desire to identify with the Jewish people, but we did believe that Jesus was the Messiah promised by Moses and the prophets.

We said then as we do now, "When the Messiah comes, we believe he will be Jesus." We talked of our understanding that the history of our faith tells us that the first followers of Jesus were all Jewish and that the early gentile converts to Jesus practiced their faith in the context of the Judaism of the day. I told him this is what we wanted to do today.

Well, to say the least, all of us were surprised. We were surprised that the issue of the Messiah came up after all these months of lessons and study classes, and the rabbi was surprised that we wanted to be Jews and yet retain our belief in Jesus. Today that concept is understood and even accepted in some quarters, but thirty plus years ago it was an anomaly. Then, the general consensus among both Christians and Jews was that you could be a Jew or a Christian, but you could not be both.

Finally, although he did not give us the conversion

papers because of our faith in Jesus, the rabbi was convinced of our genuine desire to be one with the Jewish people. After the ceremonies, he said we should at least have our marriage officially recognized by having a Jewish wedding, which we gladly did. We were also given our Jewish names, I was Jacob Ben Abraham and Patty was Miriam Ben Abraham.

The rabbi told us he would write to a learned rabbi in Israel and ask his opinion before making any final decision. A few weeks later, we were invited to his office, and he showed us a letter written in cursive Hebrew from an important Rabbi in Israel. He read it to us, translating into English as he went. The Rabbi from Israel said that he could go ahead and convert us, and in time, we would be more traditional in our views.

However, although everything required was completed, he still would not give us the official conversion papers. So we went home that day, disappointed, yet greatly enriched by a broader understanding and appreciation for the Jewish roots of our faith. We really thought at that time that this was the end of the matter as far as any official identification with the Jewish people was concerned. We were wrong, as you will see as our story unfolds.

In any case, I continued to serve as Chaplain of Wheaton College with the on-going challenges of that unique and privileged place of service. Yet with all the joy of being in such a vibrant spiritual and intellectual community, there remained a lingering hunger, a gnawing discontent. One might guess—it centered on Israel.

As the weeks and months passed, those feelings did not diminish. In the mix was a definite restlessness that I later understood was a part of the hangover from my Vietnam experience. I had yet to come to terms with the raw and jagged edges of living in a combat zone for over a year. Only combat veterans understand this. There was an unsettledness that was only exacerbated by thoughts that a quiet, academic setting might be God's terminal assignment for me. Is this it? Is this all God has for us? Even as I write this, I am ashamed to admit these feelings, since my head tells me that a person could not ask for anything more than to serve as the Chaplain of Wheaton College.

Indeed, I felt honored to have been chosen to serve in this capacity. It was a privilege to be a part of the spiritual shaping of such capable, bright young Christian students. These were the leaders of tomorrow, and I had a unique opportunity to be a part of their spiritual formation. Patty was very fulfilled and happy at Wheaton, and the children were doing well in a Christian school. What more could I ask for? In my head, I understood all I was privileged to have. In my heart, there was a hole that I began to realize could only be filled by Israel. What to do?

On the Road Again?

Since my experience at Urbana had really started the juices flowing about Jews of the first centuries retaining their identity as Jews while becoming committed followers of Jesus, I began to read more of Donald McGavren's works. In addition to his writings, Dr. McGavren had founded and become the first dean of The School of World Missions at Fuller Theological Seminary in Pasadena, California. The school had become the launching pad for McGavren's philosophy of missions or the "Church Growth" theory of how missionary effort should be conducted. Rather than the traditional mission station approach to missions, McGavren advocated the planting of churches that reflected the cultural context of the host country or people.

Again, one of his favorite examples of how that was done successfully was the first century Jewish followers of Jesus. For the most part, they had remained a part of the traditional synagogue infrastructure for at least two and a half centuries. Only when necessary had they established their own synagogues, much like Christian denominations that split today because of doctrinal divisions. But they had always remained within the cultural and religious context of their own Jewish, ethnic and religious identity.

The more I read of McGavren and his followers, the more I saw it everywhere in the pages of the New Testament, the more the vision of seeing that replicated today gripped me. It was becoming clearer. I sensed that God might be leading us to leave Wheaton and flesh out this vision through graduate studies under McGavren at Fuller Seminary.

This new and seemingly inevitable change began to be the focus of my prayers. If we were to leave Wheaton and go to Fuller Seminary, this would be another giant step of faith for our family. After all, we had only been at Wheaton for two years, and the thought of leaving after such a short time only produced more anxiety. Once again, we knew we really did need God's guidance and affirmation in this decision.

In addition to a growing sense of new direction based on God's Word, there were two factors that were important to us in making a final decision. The first was a sense of God's confirmation through the wisdom and insight of others, and the second had to do with how we would be sustained financially.

Confirmation

God's confirmation through others did, in fact, come. One source came through one of the giants of the evangelical world, Dr. Carl F.H. Henry. One of my tasks as Chaplain at Wheaton was to organize and administer the daily chapel program at the college. At that time, part of the chapel program was a three-day series of lectures by a prominent evangelical leader. They were called the Staley Memorial Lectures. This lecture series was funded by the Staley Foundation, and many Christian colleges and institutions utilized them to enhance their spiritual and educational goals.

It was with the Staley Lectures in mind that I approached

Dr. Henry in the spring of 1971 to be our lecturer for the series in the fall. I'll never forget his response. He said he would be glad to come for the series if he would be allowed to speak on the subject that he was most focused on at the time. I asked, "What subject is that?" He replied, "I don't know what it will be then, but whatever it is, that is what I will want to speak about." What could I say?

Dr. Henry was the evangelical world's Moses. I certainly didn't want to ask such a brilliant and great man to get off-focus from what he was concentrating on at the time. "Fair enough" I told him, "But so that we can properly advertise your coming, could you let us know what you will be speaking on at least thirty days before?" "Of course," he assured me. I thought one could scarcely go wrong if Dr. Carl F.H. Henry was allowed to expound on his current thinking, whatever that was. Indeed, it was a right decision.

That fall Dr. Henry came to Wheaton to give the Staley Memorial Lectures, and it was a great experience for students and faculty alike. But for our family, the most significant part of his stay at Wheaton was the family dinner we had for him at our home. We required our children to dress in their best clothes and to prepare mentally. We told them this was one of the smartest people in the world, and that they should start to think of questions to ask him. As you might expect, the conversation was unusually stimulating.

After dinner, Dr. Henry playfully rolled up his sleeves to prepare for their questions, Sarah, our eight-year-old, began by asking who Adam and Eve's children married. She and Matt had coached Rachel to ask what makes the sky blue. Matt, our ten-year-old budding scholar, began his questioning by asking Dr. Henry to explain the Trinity. It was an extraordinary evening. During the conversation, Dr. Henry gave plausible, satisfying explanations to all the questions the kids asked. It was astounding. This is a mark of a true intellectual—the capacity to explain great truths in a way that a child can understand—which, of course, is what Jesus could do and, in fact, did do on many occasions.

For Patty and me, however, one of the highlights of the evening came after the children were prayed with and tucked in bed, when we shared with Dr. Henry our experience in Israel, our love for the Jewish people and our attempt to identify with them through a ceremonial conversion. We went through the whole experience, blow by blow, up to and including our refusal to sign the document renouncing all former faiths with their messianic and theological tenants.

Dr. Henry sat quietly through the whole story, listening intently, nodding approvingly from time to time. Then all of sudden he stopped us and raised his hand, "Let me pray," he said. He bowed his head and after a silence that seemed to go on forever, he finally prayed, "Yes, Lord, this is of You, this is of God. May Your empowering grace and blessing rest on this family as they follow Your extraordinary leading. Yes, this is of God! In Jesus' name, Amen."

Certainly, Dr. Henry's response was the kind of confirmation that we were seeking for the difficult decision that was becoming more and more inevitable. To say the least, we were greatly encouraged to have a man of the spiritual stature of Dr. Carl F.H. Henry affirm what we sensed to be God's leading. Additional confirmation came in the person of one the most beloved members of Wheaton's faculty.

Dr. Samuel J. Schultz was Professor of Bible and Theology and chairman of the Division of Biblical Studies at Wheaton College. He was the author of the highly acclaimed book, *The Old Testament Speaks,* as well as many other Old Testament related books. We had become good friends primarily as a result of our mutual interest in Israel and matters related to the teaching and culture of the Hebrew Scriptures.

Sam had walked with us through the whole conversion process and found the classes I would share with him to be stimulating to his own understanding of his chosen field of study. He, too, affirmed the approach we were taking in attempting to identify, as fully as possible, with the Jewish people. In a sense, he navigated with us through the uncharted waters of the course we were taking. His fellowship and prayers became continuing affirmations of the path we were following.

Finally, I was one of a group of three men that met regularly for prayer, personal sharing, accountability and fellowship. I shared with them not only of the conversion process, but also of God's guidance for us to leave Wheaton and go to Fuller Seminary. Don "Bubba" Church was the head track couch and assistant football coach at Wheaton and a man of unusual spiritual maturity and insight. I highly valued his discernment.

The other man in the trio was Dr. Ralph Alexander, Professor of Old Testament in the Bible Department. He and his wife Myrna were dear friends of longstanding, going all the way back to Dallas Seminary days. It was their wisdom and counsel together with regular, intercessory prayer that became the needed final confirmation we needed to actually make a move.

Watchmen on the Walls

One major consideration was left—how would we pay for graduate school and support a family of five with my studying full time. I had not used my GI Bill options, which turned out to make the difference for us. I looked at a number of organizations and even a denomination or two, but found none of them to have the same vision for Israel that we had. So, on the advice and counsel of a number of friends, including an attorney, we decided to start a 501(c)(3), non-profit organization. Thus was born *The Watchmen Association*, taken from Isaiah 62:6-7, *"I have posted watchmen on your walls, O Jerusalem; they will never be silent day or night. You who call on the name of the Lord, give yourselves no rest, and give him now rest till he establishes Jerusalem and makes her the praise of all the earth.*"

We prepared a small list of friends and family and wrote to them of our decision to leave Wheaton and go to Fuller Seminary for their doctoral program in the School of World Missions. We asked them to prayerfully consider supporting us financially through the studies program. We told them that if the Lord opened the door, we wanted to return to Israel. Although the IRS ruled not to allow support for the personal expenses of schooling, with the GI Bill, part time work and a small group of loyal friends and family, it was possible for us to reach our goal. To them we remain deeply grateful. The decision was made. We were off to California to study Cross-Cultural Studies.

At this point in our pilgrimage, I can say that I "saw through a glass darkly." I wanted to be involved with Israel and the Jewish people and was not completely clear about how that would play out. I believed that we were nearing what the Bible calls "the latter days" and I read what everyone else read in the Bible—that at some point, "All Israel will be saved." What did that mean? Who was "all Israel?" Saved from what? Would it be with miraculous intervention on God's part, as it was with Paul and the apostles? Would it be through genuine, open discussions and seminars that understanding, salvation and restoration would take place?

When I first came to faith in Jesus, I thought Israel would be saved as I had—by becoming cultural Christians. In time, I began to really grasp the fact that the first believers were very Jewish. Since the establishment of the State of Israel and the opening up of the Jewish roots to our faith, a new understanding and emphasis, which I think is more biblical, has emerged. Today, I believe that I see better, more from His perspective, the process God has to bring people into a relationship with Himself. Let me explain.

Today, and especially since my involvement with *encouraging Christians to stand with Israel,* I readily heed the Apostle Peter's admonition, *"Always be prepared to give an answer to everyone who asks you to give the reason for the hope that you have. But do this with gentleness and respect"* (I Peter 3:15). Having said that, I have come to realize that I, personally, cannot change anyone's heart. I cannot convert anyone to anything. Only God, by His grace, can change anyone. Even Jesus said that one has to be "born from above." Only God, by His Holy Spirit, can touch a human heart. Jesus said it best: *"No one can come to me unless the Father who sent me draws him, and I will raise him up at the last day ...no one can come to me unless the Father has enabled him"* (John 6:44, 65). So, we are to give witness of our faith to all people as we are asked and have opportunity, knowing that it is God, exercising of His sovereign will, who moves on individual hearts.

The Witness of Love

But is that all we can do? No, there's more. And here I must revert back to the vision implanted by Dr. G. Douglas Young during our first stay in Jerusalem in 1969-70 at the American Institute of Holy Land Studies. His passion was to establish relationships with the Jewish people based on genuine friendship, concern, trust and understanding—not to come at them with a hidden motive of evangelizing them. Rather, we are to believe in the power of love. We are to simply love our Jewish friends and let relationships take their natural courses under God's providential oversight.

The Apostle Paul apparently had this in mind when he spoke of his *"hope that I may somehow arouse my own people to envy"* (Romans 10:19; 11:11, 14). And how does one arouse another to envy and a good jealousy? Again Paul gives us the answer, *"Just as you were at one time disobedient to*

*God have now received mercy as a result of their disobedi-
ence, so they too have now become disobedient in order that
they too may now receive mercy as a result of God's mercy to
you"* (Romans 11:30-31). Therefore, God's mandate to
Christians in relationships with Jews is to show mercy
because of the mercy Christians have received through Jesus
Christ. The Christian is to initiate and attempt to maintain a
relationship, displaying genuine concern, acts of compassion
and solidarity that can build trustworthy and lasting relationships.

Now is a good time to add an important observation
regarding the Christian's relationship to Jews. I have noted
the importance of showing mercy because of mercy
received. As a matter of fact, we state this as God's mandate
for our ministry in standing with Israel. Having said that,
however, I don't mean we are to concoct some manufactured
notion of mercy and love for the Jewish people—quite the
contrary. If and when something phony or lacking heartfelt
sincerity is directed toward the Jews, they are the first to recognize it. If it's only their souls you want, Jews have an
uncanny capacity to pick up on that.

On the other hand, I have observed over the years that
those who have a genuine love for Israel and the Jewish people do so because God has implanted that love and desire to
stand up and identify with them. It is a call and capacity that
transcends denominations, organizations and cultures. It can
only be explained as a gift from God. It is not based on
whether or not Jews accept us or our beliefs. It is unconditional, even in the face of rejection. It is not conditional on
the response of Jews. So, in that sense, it is a human reflection of the love of God. It is specifically a reflection of the
love of Jesus, because the Bible declares, *"While we were
still sinners, Christ died for us"* (Romans 5:8).

In any case, our strong desire to identify and stand in
unity with the Jewish people had come to the point of deci-

sion. We were going to Fuller Theological Seminary.

When I informed Dr. Armerding, the President of Wheaton College, of our decision, his initial response was one of surprise. We had only been back at Wheaton for two years. Wheaton was simply not a place one leaves, especially given the position I had as the Chaplain. But on reflection, our good friend Dr. Armerding, saw that our decision was of God and he provided a wonderful and blessed send-off for us.

Dr. Armerding remains in my thinking as one of the greatest spiritual leaders of our time. He certainly was all of that and more to the Hutchens' family. So after several days of packing and good byes it was...

California, here we come! But, first some words from Patty.

Patty's Perspective

Loving the Hebrew Language

As soon as we had gotten back to Wheaton, I began to hang around the art department at the college and almost immediately went to sign up for a course in biblical Hebrew. Dr. Barton Payne, who later was killed when he fell off a mountain, was my professor. I can say without hesitation that he was one of the greatest teachers I have ever known. I came home after the first day in class almost gasping for breath with excitement. From the day my mother told me, "A day without learning is lost forever," that is the way learning has affected me.

I told Jim, "Jim, you won't believe it. Dr. Payne says there is nothing to learning biblical Hebrew. He said all you have to do is learn the verb system and vocabulary." Jim paused for a moment or two and responded, "Patty, that's all there is to learning any language." I let that remark roll off my back. No one was going to put a damper on my love for the Hebrew language.

At any rate, since taking Hebrew in Ulpan most of the year we lived in Israel, I had been captivated with the language. Studying and reading stories in first year French was just homework. Nothing happened in my spirit. Now, here I was after just a few weeks of Hebrew, reading the first few verses of *Genesis* in the Bible. If I had known about it before, I might have majored in Hebrew or archaeology, since very few things are more exciting to me than struggling to read an old shard from 3,000 years ago, or pouring over pictures of daggers and seals with early Hebrew letters carved on them.

So after plunging into Hebrew for two years in Wheaton's graduate school, I was nominated for and elected to the National Scholastic Honor Society. I have said many times since that *all* children would be in Honor Societies if they could only link up with learning something they loved. Later, I would combine the love of Hebrew and art, but that is for another time.

All the time while studying Hebrew and trying to be a good mother and chaplain's wife, I was also studying art at the Chicago Art Institute, trekking down to The Windy City on the commuter train with huge canvases and boxes of art supplies. Rain or shine, I went. Chicago is very predictable. It's always windy. It's usually rainy. If not rainy, then at least gray, wet, cold, damp, humid or snowy. The supplies and I were usually covered from head to toe with one of Jim's big Army slickers.

For a nice lunch break, I usually went outside and walked around Chicago, a city I had come to love for reasons I cannot really explain. Like a mother loves her child. They say that everything in the world can be found in Chicago . . . and people who love it just love it. After one long lunch break walk, I found myself in front of a synagogue. Feeling quite at home, I went in to discover a few men having a noontime service. Off to the side were a few women with prayer books, some engaged in reading, others talking. I knew this was normal.

I quietly covered my head, and joined the ladies and started trying to plow my way through the Hebrew. I recognized all the "Baruch Ata, Adonai, Eloheinu" passages, and continued reading until time to return to art class. After that, I began to drop in occasionally and each time found reading the Hebrew prayers a little easier. One day I noticed a sign for those interested in conversion, asked about it, took down some information and shared it with Jim later that evening.

Truly, if I had known the firestorm that our efforts and actions would cause, I would never have considered going to a single class. I would not have given Jim the notice. I realized later that I had lived a sheltered life, but never in my life had I been acquainted with animosity either from Jews toward Christians or from Christians toward Jews. In my family, it would have been unheard of to be against Jews.

It may be difficult for some people to understand that, but where I grew up and with only one Jewish family in town, the issue we dealt with was relations between blacks and whites. Although I wish I could report that I did not hear the "N" word frequently in my growing up years, at least my parents never said negative or hurtful things about anybody. Blacks were in a ghetto on the other side of our town. As much as I can recall, I never even once met a young black person my age. There was a dear, beloved black man, Marshall, who was at my home in the country almost all day, every day. He and Daddy farmed our fifty-plus acres. Part of the farm was called "The Big Bear Den," and part was called "The Little Bear Den." They fished in our Daddy-made and well-stocked fishpond. Both our families lived off the harvests. Sometimes, they set up a little stand by the side of the Atlanta Road and sold fresh corn and vegetables. And when they slaughtered a cow or pig, Daddy drove Marshall to his home on the other side of town with sacks full of meat just like we had laying around on tables on the back porch. We loved Marshall and I know that he loved me and my family.

Once when I was about nine years old, as we were preparing dinner in our little farmhouse with no furniture in the tiny living room, I set a plate down and said, "This plate is for Marshall." My Daddy never even looked up, but quietly informed me, "Marshall won't eat in here, baby."

"Why?" I asked in disbelief.

"He doesn't like to eat inside; he likes to eat on the porch," Daddy said.

So I proceeded to take my plate and told my Mama and Daddy, "I'm eating outside with Marshall. I don't like to eat inside either."

When I went outside and asked Marshall why he didn't like to eat inside, he just said, "I don't know, Miss Patty, I just like to eat outside."

"Can I eat with you, Marshall?"

"Of course you can, Miss Patty."

The issues became deeper, darker and not so simple as the years passed, but I have always been grateful that my parents somehow walked me through those years without ever having taught me bigotry or hate. I left home and went north to Chicago to an integrated Wheaton College, just before the upheavals that would eventually bring the beginnings of integration and equal rights.

But in regard to Jews, my knowledge was theoretical; it was from the Bible. And I knew my Bible. I had read it backwards and forward from my youth, and although I read that some religious Jews in high places had come against Jesus, I didn't find that implausible. We were in the heart of Long Country. My grandmother was the sister of Huey Long, the Kingfish, the Governor of Louisiana and I *had* been raised on politics.

In Louisiana, at least where I lived, there were two parties. There were The Longs. And there were the Anti-Longs. I was led to believe they were all relatives, and somebody was always coming against somebody. Mama said everything was political, and I was instructed to keep my mouth shut about politics at school if I wanted to succeed. I can't personally say whether I ever met a Republican or not until I left Louisiana and went to Illinois. I do recall that when some folks in Illinois heard me say something nice about Democrats, they were shocked.

When I met the extended family of my husband-to-be, almost the first thing they asked me was my political affiliation. I thought they would be more interested in my religion. When these Indiana Quakers heard that Jim was dating a Democrat from Louisiana, most of them had serious doubts, but I guess they hoped we would manage to work it out and we did.

So although some Jews had perhaps even hated Jesus, I also knew that most of the people who followed Jesus were Jews. All my heroes were Jewish. In fact, both the good guys and the bad guys were Jewish.

While we went through the classes and conversion in Chicago on one hand and went to church and chapel at Wheaton on the other, it was rather fascinating. My mother had always told me that I could read anything and consider anything, so I had a rather fearless approach to learning. I was never put off much by people who disagreed with me either politically or religiously. If I had been a man, I could have sat for hours in Athens and discussed great issues with the scholars, if I'd been Greek — somewhat like Daddy used to say, "If we had bacon—we'd have bacon and eggs—if we had eggs." We all knew he wasn't talking about either bacon or eggs. This was one of those teaching things they did without ever talking about the real things.

Here we were now, without bacon or eggs, scrambling to

make a living, trying to be Christian, trying to be Jewish, trying to learn Hebrew, trying to raise a family, trying out new ideas, trying to follow Jesus better, and trying to get over Vietnam. We had no idea what lay ahead. But does anybody know what lies ahead?

One thing I did know: We were going back to being poor. Jim promised if he got this doctorate, it would be his last school. So we kept on trying and moving ahead—not knowing that God's greatest adventures for us still lay ahead.

CHAPTER 8

On to Academia:
The Seminary and the Synagogue

O ur move from Wheaton to Pasadena was a character-building experience. Across the western desert in July in a Ryder truck with no air-conditioning reminded me somewhat of combat days in the jungles of Vietnam. Matt and I, along with our collie Wellington, manned the truck. Patty and the girls were crammed into our station wagon with additional necessary household goods.

I have this thing about traveling. Some say it's part of the male psyche. I just want to keep on going—to press on until we reach our destination. For some reason, those of the female persuasion don't seem to share that passion. Those two dynamics were at work between Patty and me from the time we left Wheaton until we arrived in Pasadena.

We were less than forty miles from Pasadena when Patty began signaling me with her lights to stop. We pulled to the side of the road. As I went back to the car, I was greeted with, "We're exhausted—I can't stay awake any longer—we have to stop!"

"But we're less than forty miles from Pasadena," I offered unconvincingly.

"You go on ahead; we're stopping!" Of course, this brought the discussion to an end. We found the closest motel.

I must confess that the next day did look brighter after a good night's sleep. Our first day in Pasadena was spent checking into the Seminary and getting the necessary information for the upcoming fall semester orientation. We also got some prospects for housing from the Seminary, but actually found the newspaper classifieds to be the most help. Our search for housing didn't take long.

Kosher Home

On the second day we found a wonderful place to rent in Altadena, right next to Pasadena. The home was owned by an orthodox Jewish man. The kitchen was even fitted with two ovens and a proper Sabbath warmer on the stove. (Religious Jews aren't supposed to light a fire on the Sabbath.) Even more interesting, the closest house of worship was a Conservative Synagogue a few blocks away. Was God saying something to us? We concluded He was and began attending services regularly. Since services were held on Friday evening and Saturday morning, we occasionally visited churches in the area on Sunday. We had the best of both worlds.

However, Friday evening Shabbat services became very special to us. Indeed, it was a growing delight to be a part of this Sabbath experience. There was a strange sense in which we felt we were being connected for the first time to our own original spiritual roots. Our faith in Jesus was even enhanced as we began to see the cultural and spiritual context out of which He came. And, as we have learned over the years, it is that same Jewish context that served as our own spiritual moorings as Christians.

This was where we began to learn the sequence and importance of the prayers and songs of the Jewish Prayer Book. I had taken four years of Hebrew in my first seminary training and at least knew how to read the text, be it ever so slowly. Still, I found it difficult to speak. Patty, on the other hand, had learned to speak Hebrew fairly well from our initial stay in Israel by talking to neighborhood women and children and conversing at the market. Both of us had studied at an Ulpan—a conversational Hebrew studies program. So she was able to read, speak and write.

As a result of our involvement in synagogue activities, the next two years were an immersion experience in cultural Judaism. This period of time remains a vital part of our life to this day. The rabbi and those who knew us in the congregation knew that I was enrolled in studies at Fuller Theological Seminary. Fuller had a good reputation in the Jewish community because they were very involved in the Jewish-Christian dialogue that was then current. In the seminary list of students, my faith was listed as Jewish.

There were questions, as you might expect, on the part of some wanting to know who we were and what we were doing there. I remember one conversation in which a woman said, "Now, Hutchens—that's not a Jewish name, is it?"

"No" I said, "But we both have Jews in our background." Not only is that true for us, but it is probably true of most of us. I went on to say, "We are excited about being able to explore our Jewish roots." While we told anyone who asked if we believed Jesus to be the Messiah, the fact is that we were attending all the services and the social events and participating fully in synagogue life. We did not experience a single slight or difficult time in this very progressive synagogue. I think most assumed that we more and more considered ourselves to be Jewish.

I found our acceptance especially encouraging when I attended the Saturday morning Torah Services. For the first several months, I would attend this all-male service on Saturday mornings and simply sit through the service, learning the procedure. Then, on a number of occasions, I was asked to come to the Bema, the raised platform where the Torah (the first five books of the Old Testament) was placed, and offer the prayers before and after the reading of that Sabbath's portion.

At first, I was hesitant because I didn't know how to read Hebrew well and I hadn't learned some of the regular prayers. But over time, and after much encouragement from the men in the service, I was able to memorize the prayers in Hebrew and was eager to take part. It is a distinct honor to be called to the Bema and to participate in the reading of God's Word. I considered it an honor then and I do so today, as well.

Recognizing this active involvement in the synagogue for our whole family, we were approached about joining the synagogue. We told those who encouraged us to join that we were not officially Jews, but that we had undergone all the necessary training for conversion to Judaism. I told them that I would write to the rabbi who had conducted our instruction and see what he had to say.

I then wrote to the rabbi in Chicago and told him how our whole family was very much involved the life of this synagogue and that we were being encouraged to officially join. I asked if there was anything he could provide us to show that we had actually completed the course of pre-scribed study. To say the least, we were shocked at his reply.

In about ten days, we were glad to receive by return mail the official documents from the Chicago Rabbinate saying we had met all the requirements for conversion to Judaism. In addition, it cited the fact that we had been married according to Jewish law and included the official papers with our Hebrew names. Nothing had changed since our last day with the rabbi, but I think he sent us the official conversion document because he genuinely believed we were really willing to identify ourselves as Jews and adopt a distinctively Jewish lifestyle, kosher and all.

It was an act of good faith on his part. And he was absolutely right. We were indeed willing and ready to do just that. I did not then, nor do I now, think that such a commitment conflicts with believing in Jesus. It certainly did not when all this began in the first century. The first believing community was made up of thousands of Jews—only Jews—believing in a Jew about whom only Jews had written. However, it remains a tragic reality that over time, followers of Jesus either were separated or separated themselves from their heritage. After the destruction of Jerusalem in AD 70 and the dispersion of the Jews and after persecution and bitterness, it was almost inevitable.

As I think about this now thirty years later, I can say that I could still adopt a Jewish lifestyle. I believe that was the lifestyle of the first followers of Jesus and, if I understand the Scriptures correctly, that is part of what Jesus will restore when He returns. (cf. Matthew 19:28; Acts 3:21). For years, I have contended that the future faith of the followers of Jesus will be marked by a distinctively Jewish lifestyle. For example, the Sabbath and many biblical festivals will be restored as a part of the worship agenda of true believers. (cf. Isaiah 66:23, Zechariah 14:16-19).

In any case, the fact that we had an official and legitimate conversion document in our possession opened all kinds of possibilities for the future. The first was the possibility of joining the synagogue that we had grown to love and respect. The second was the possibility of going back to Israel and actually becoming citizens under the Law of Return. The Law of Return, at that time, held that any Jew who comes to Israel could gain automatic citizenship because he was returning to his God-ordained ancestral homeland. He is returning from his exile in the Diaspora and thus, after due process, receives citizenship in the State of Israel.

Acting on the conversion document, we joined the synagogue and got even more involved. I was invited to take part in an adult Bar Mitzvah ceremony where a number of men who were either converts or had never gone through a Bar

Mitzvah in their youth, took part in this time honored rite of passage. In addition, I was asked to head up the synagogue Social Committee. This group oversaw the family potluck/cookout and swim outings that our family had participated in during the summer months. It was a gracious gesture on the part of the synagogue leadership to recognize our involvement and to include us in a low-level position of responsibility.

All in all, our experience in the life and worship of the synagogue was positive and enriching and one we cherish to this day. However, since I had come to California to involve myself in a doctoral study program, it was important to be about the task.

A Breakthrough Dissertation

The Fuller Seminary School of World Mission has now been renamed the School of Intercultural Studies because of the negative connotation of the word "mission" in some cultures. Wheaton College, likewise, has changed their mascot name from "Crusaders," a name that can put barriers between those who seek to live out the principles Jesus taught and those who don't.

This whole concept of cultural sensitivity is a reflection of Dr. Donald McGavren's philosophy of missions, which had drawn me to the school. The program of study was designed especially for those who had been in ministry, in the field usually for a period of years, and had faced many of the inevitable problems, especially culturally related problems that arise during service. The School sought to provide a mid-career problem-solving experience for students. The student's thesis or dissertation was then directed toward a significant issue or problem which he or she had encountered in the field. The end product was to be an exercise in problem-solving. It was a very practical and appealing approach to graduate education.

As I mentioned earlier, a capsule summary of McGavren's philosophy of missions was in the statement, *"Men like to become Christians* (today we would say 'believers') *without crossing racial, linguistic, or class barriers."* (McGavren,1970, page198) Of course, McGavren's prototype model for this was the Jewish community of Jesus' day. Because the Jews who believed in Jesus did not have to "cross racial, linguistic or class barriers" to become His followers, the multitudes followed Him.

Only a fraction of the religious leadership came against Jesus and even this resistance was restrained because of fear of a backlash from the masses. (Matthew 14:5, 26:1-5) Rather, His following grew exponentially among Jews. On the day of Pentecost *"About three thousand were added to their number that day"* (Acts 2:41). Only a few days after that, *"the number of men grew to about five thousand"* (Acts 4:4). And the body of believers continued to grow unabated, *"So the Word of God spread. The number of disciples in Jerusalem increased rapidly, and a large number of priests became obedient to the faith"* (Acts 6:7).

And how do we account for this phenomenal growth? A major factor has to be that Jews didn't have to cease being Jews to follow Jesus. Their identity as Jews was never in question. *"Everyday they continued to meet together in the Temple"* (Acts 2:46, 5:21, 42).

They continued to attend the synagogue on the Sabbath: *"On the Sabbath they entered the synagogue and sat down. After the reading from the Law and Prophets . . ."* (Acts 13:14). Even the Apostle Paul continued to keep the purification rites. *"The next day Paul took the men and purified himself along with them. Then he went to the temple to give notice of the date when the days of purification would end and the offering would be made for each of them"* (Acts 21:26).

These were specifically Jewish religious acts. The leadership of Jerusalem believers even boasted to Paul, *"You see,* *brother, how many **thousands of Jews** have believed and **all of them are zealous of the law**"* (Acts 21:20).

As an aside, the accusations of anti-Semitism in Mel Gibson's film, *The Passion of Christ*, comes from a massive misreading, even a distortion of the Gospels and the book of Acts. The Jews as a people did not reject Jesus. As a matter of factual record, the multitudes followed Him. As I have noted above, only a small minority of the religious leadership came against Him, and even then on the sly, for fear the people would rise up in riot against them. Every religion has political issues within the religious establishment.

There are three important biblical factors that must be considered with respect to the death of Jesus.

(1) Jesus laid down His own life. No one took it from Him. *"I lay down my life—only to take it up again. No one takes it from me, but I lay it down of my own accord. I have authority to lay it down and authority to take it up again"* (John 10:17-18).

(2) In His own words, Jesus predicts the complicity of a minority of the Jewish religious establishment, but says that the Gentiles were guilty of actually putting Him to death. *"We are going to Jerusalem, and the Son of Man will be betrayed to the chief priests and the teachers of the Law. They will condemn him to death and will turn him over to the **Gentiles** to be mocked and flogged and crucified. On the third day he will be raised to life"* (Matthew 20:18). It is important to note that the death of Jesus was not final. The tomb was empty after three days. Jesus rose from the dead! Hallelujah! And further,

(3) According to the Scriptures, the guilt and culpability for Jesus' death must be shared by all—Jew and Gentile alike. *"Indeed Herod and Pontius Pilate met together with the Gentiles and the people of Israel in this city to conspire against your holy servant Jesus, who you [**God**] anointed. They did what **your power** and **will foreordained** to happen"*

(Acts 4:27-28).

The fact of the matter is that God predestined the death of Jesus. Herod, Pontius Pilate, Jews and Gentiles were simply the means God used to bring it about. Finally, anyone who comes to faith through Jesus knows that *his or her own sins* were part of the reason Jesus laid down His life. Somehow all these relevant factors have been lost in the heat of rhetorical exchange. But I have digressed.

With McGaven's insight in mind, I began to see with more clarity the problem I wanted to address. The challenge was that of recapturing and replicating the context of faith of the first century followers of Jesus. It worked then, why not today? Fortunately for me, the man assigned as mentor for my dissertation shared my passion. He was none other than the Dean of the School of World Mission, Dr. Arthur F. Glasser. I shall be eternally grateful for the patient and prodding oversight he gave to my work. He brought a unique blend of academic excellence and spiritual integrity to his critique of my efforts. We met only a few times when it was agreed what I would write on—*A Case for Messianic Judaism.*

As I look back, probably a better title would have been *A Case for Nazarene Judaism,* for that is, in fact, closer to what I was referring. Acts 24:5 speaks of Paul as the ringleader of the Nazarene sect. The followers of "The Way," as they were often referred to (Acts 19:9, 23, 22:4, 24:14, 22), were called the Nazarene sect of Judaism, much as the sects of the Pharisees or Sadducees. They were not known as Christians. The term *Christian* is only used three times in the New Testament. (cf. Acts 11:26, 26:28, I Peter 4:16). In any case, the followers of Jesus were considered under the umbrella of Judaism, certainly not outside its pale. My dissertation would attempt to demonstrate this from the Bible and encourage its replication today. In the preface I stated:

"The call today to both Jew and Christian is to a reevaluation of the basic issues. What are those issues? Broadly speaking there are two:

>   (1) **A core-faith**. The Scriptures point to and articulate a core-faith that is essential to spiritual life and resident in all the people of God. It comes as divine revelation. It is non-negotiable.
>   (2) **A cultural dress**. This is the variable. Both Judaism and Christianity have their distinctive cultural manifestations. These are relative as opposed to being divinely revealed. With this perspective we shall seek, if possible, to articulate a new resolution and a new option for the people of God, whether Jewish or Christian.

This position will encourage and allow for the acceptance of Jesus as Lord, Messiah, and Redeemer by Jewish people, while maintaining their cultural and religious identity as Jews. Hopefully, we shall also call Gentile Christians to adopt a more biblical perspective and lifestyle in their calling to serve Jesus as Lord and Savior."

A Case for Messianic Judaism was written in 1974 at the very beginning of the Messianic movement. I predicted its growth would be in direct proportion to the number and quality of Messianic congregations that would be planted and maintained. That, in fact, has been the case.

Today there are scores of Messianic congregations across

America and the world, for that matter, including Israel. Many Jewish believers have found safe haven in such congregations. At the same time, they have often been anathematized by many in the Jewish religious establishment. Unfortunately, Jesus remains the barrier issue for many Jews. Unexpectedly, there have been large numbers of Gentile believers who have flocked to these congregations, primarily in search of the Hebrew foundational roots to their faith.

Now, with my academic studies completed in the spring of 1974, it was decision time once again. Should we return to Israel and attempt to fully identify with the Jewish people by applying for citizenship under the Law of Return? We had a legitimate conversion document in our hands. Our heart for Israel had only increased. Our vision to be a part of the land, the people and the culture had greatly enlarged. Israel was beckoning. Let's go for it! But wait. Let Patty prepare the way.

Patty's Perspective

All I could think about on the endless trip to California were the poor, unfortunate women who had married men in the Gold Rush days. I even thought quite a bit about the Children of Israel in the wilderness, or more specifically, the women of Israel. First of all, we had an old station wagon. The girls and I thought that we were more fortunate when we considered that Jim, Matt and the dog were in the U-Haul. Wellington, our thoroughbred dog, went the entire trip from Illinois to California with his head hanging out the window, gasping for breath.

I often wondered if that wasn't the reason he got some serious disease and died not too long after we got to Pasadena. Seriously, has anyone ever driven across the desert in an old car that has only a small amount of Freon in the air-conditioning? And did anyone ever willingly go with a man who wanted to stop only every 500 miles for water and necessities? And wanted to drive all day and all night? I was a seriously healthy and courageous young woman, but the fact that Jim and I were still married at the end of this trip was, I thought, quite unusual. At first, I tried to cooperate. Occasionally, I had to take matters in my own hands.

Finally, the girls and I decided that when we saw a little store or gas station, we would start blowing our horn to signal Jim to stop. We had no idea when the next stop would be. After driving a few hours, the station wagon began to heat up, which any normal thing would do in the blazing hot sun of the desert. Not too long into the trip, I figured that if I taped paper and completely covered all the windows, except for just a little space to see through to drive, we would be cooler. I was right. I assumed that anyone behind me would come around on the left lane and I could see for miles any car that was going in the other direction. I'm sure that was against the law, but I was confident that highway patrolmen had more sense than to drive in that heat. After we figured out this unique "cooling system," even Matt and the dog wanted to be with us.

We did stop for the night once in the middle of the trip. I will not even go into the Sleep Cheap hotel we stayed in, but it was cool and we did rest. True, as we were nearing our destination, I insisted that we stop for the night. I was so groggy I could no longer stay on the road. My sweet Sarah was so nervous about me running off the road that she kept talking to me quite loudly and feeding me popcorn.

We went on for at least two hours in that condition. Finally something snapped, and I made a quality decision on the spot. I pulled over and dropped back my head while Sarah laid on the horn. Although Jim did not stop right away, as he got farther and farther away, he realized we were not going to start back up, no matter how long he hung his arm out the window and signaled us to come on. When he finally got back to the car, Sarah said, "Dad,

Mom is asleep."

We got to Pasadena the next day, found our little house soon afterward and moved in. We had moved so many times by now that I told Jim, "When we leave California, I will not have a single friend; then there would be no good-byes." Years later, Sarah would tell me that she thought I had an abandonment complex . . . and I think she was right. I never liked leaving anywhere we lived. I never wanted to give away the cars we had driven. I kept all the little clothes the children had when they were babies. So leaving Wheaton was as traumatic as all our moves had been.

After we had packed up and everyone else was in the truck and car, I had dropped down on the kitchen floor and sobbed, so sad to leave my friends and my safe place in the world. But, now here we were in California; and all of us took to it immediately and settled in for two wonderful years. We walked to the synagogue each Shabbat and for special events. We had Shabbat dinners in our kosher kitchen and soon were inviting friends from the synagogue for matzo ball soup and my special beef brisket.

The small dining room of the house we rented was Jim's office. As I had done in Dallas, I typed all his papers. Back in Dallas, he was not allowed even an erasure on his final thesis, but here in California, they were more generous. Years later, I would finally give him a computer and insist that the time had come for him to start typing his own papers. Of course, with the ease of making changes and corrections on a computer, it was easy.

However, one advantage of all that typing through the years was that I read and re-read every idea he ever wrote and studied from all the Scriptures. So we both ended up with almost the same education, two for the price of one.

Our Jewish Connection

Jim was listed in the Seminary phone list as Jewish, and

we fit in quite normally in the synagogue life. I found celebrating true biblical feasts and festivals quite rewarding personally and spiritually. We never took part in Halloween again, and what everyone says they want to do at Christmas and Easter, we did. Instead of decorations that have absolutely no spiritual connection, we concentrated on Jesus' birth and resurrection within a biblical context. We didn't put a blinking Santa in the front yard, and as we had done when we lived in Israel, we really celebrated and practiced the Sabbath. I mean we didn't work or cut the grass. We didn't clean or paint the house. We didn't go shopping or do all the hundred other things that have gotten crammed into the Christian Sunday. We did what God did on the Sabbath. We rested. Not only did we prepare all the food before sundown on Friday, but we stopped all work and concentrated on being with the family, listening to spiritual music, reading the Bible and having family discussions.

We took casual walks and rested. We didn't even answer the phone. We started a practice of not having desserts during the week and then having one very special dessert Friday night. No one can imagine what it is like to practice the Sabbath until they have done it for a few weeks or months. Something wonderful happens. Somewhere along the middle of the week, you begin to long for it. You begin to be stronger and more energetic, able to get more done on the other six days because you know for sure you will rest on the Sabbath. And I think God just blesses you for it. He said He would.

I remembered that as a child we had practiced a similar life style in my family. We went to church in the morning and then went home and ate food that had been cooked the day before. Everyone took a nap and stayed around the house the whole day. No stores were open, so there was no temptation to go anywhere. In my family we did not go to movies on Sunday nor did we iron or do any work. It was the one day of the week when my Daddy did only what had to be done on the farm, like feed the horse. No fishing, no hunting, no playing dominoes or checkers.

Many Americans used to practice the Sabbath on Sunday and we were better off for it. Now most people go ninety-to-nothing seven days a week, and Sunday is like any other day. For the majority of Jews, Saturday is like any other day. It is a great loss for us individually and as a nation.

As I had always done everywhere we had lived, I took art classes. This time I went to Pasadena City College and took drawing and printmaking. It's amazing how something as simple as deciding to take an etching course can open up an entirely new world. Although I took courses in printmaking after California, the two years with Ben Sacaguchi at Pasadena were to affect my life for years to come. I began to do etchings that were related to biblical themes. He was a highly motivating teacher, and a complete master of every method of this art form.

During World War II, Ben had been placed with his family in one of those Japanese camps we set up in our country. He freely talked about it; he was not bitter and had gone on to be a great teacher and artist. I could speak to him from my heart about Jewish issues and the mix with Jesus. Of course, artists are always the first people to consider new ideas. Tell an artist he can't do something—that is exactly what he will do.

I had begun to get a picture of cross-cultural issues after my own personal history, and did not even flinch with the idea of living in the Jewish culture and believing in Jesus. I was well aware of how "wrong headed" many "mission" efforts had been in the past. I had a friend at Wheaton whose father had made a huge cultural leap in South America.

When he had first gone to South America, he did what everyone did. He lived in a gated compound at night and went out among the "natives" during the day. After a few years, his wife, the mother of my friend, died there. A year or so later, her father married a native woman. He was immediately dismissed from his denomination, as it did not allow marrying a native or living with one. What happened is a good example of what does happen when racial and cultural barriers are broken down. This man and his "native" wife, who spoke several dialects and shared his faith, took the truth of their faith to many tribes of people, where they made an enormous impact.

I heard about a man who went to a tribal group that had never even seen a white person. However, he lived in the trees as they did, wore a loin clothe as they did, married a local woman and proceeded to be a permanent part of a complete people movement to faith in God. The day is coming, if it is not here already, when we will wake up to the fact that we have built walls around people and fenced ourselves out and them in—or fenced ourselves in and them out.

I believe that Jesus really represented that new approach in His day. He was actually speaking as a Jew to Jews and saying that the masses of people were shut out by religious systems that privileged a few. Do we not see that today? Why does that seem so strange when almost every denomination and or organization on earth has to deal with these problems? Were the Jews of Jesus'day the only people in the world who had no rotten eggs among them? Were there no high minded, self-righteous people then? Were there no greedy, self-serving hypocrites who thought only of themselves and were interested only in protecting their own self interests?

Look at the history of people, much less religion. Jews are no different from the Irish, the English, Africans or Asians in this respect. Look at Israel today. Everyone knows that Israel has its share of criminals, prostitutes, mafia, religious feuds, tax evaders, drunk drivers and whatever else there is—just like the rest of the world.

The problem is the same problem when anyone any-where looks at any group of people in a monolithic way. When we were still in the shameful time of segregation in America, much less slavery before that, any time a black person looked at someone crossways, they were accused of horrible crimes and treated despicably. Public humiliation and a complete system of ghetto life and ostracizing were the norm. The best possible thing that America can do is just admit it and vow to fight for justice for all. The worst possible thing is to deny it and to pretend that white people are incapable of evil.

I believe the day will come when normal Israelis will look back and see that there were some lemons in the leadership at the time of Jesus. They will see that Jesus was a Jewish problem and that He was unjustly treated by some of the religious hierarchy. They will claim as their own the New Testament, books written almost entirely by Jews to Jews about a Jew. I believe the day will come when Israelis will refuse to be told what they can think, do and believe, and will come to their own conclusions about one of their own.

But Jews have not really been free to think about Jesus in a normal way for two thousand years because of the horrific anti-Semitism that has driven an iron wedge between them and Jesus. It is similar to what might have happened in this country because of slavery and segregation. The incredible, successful and non-violent leadership of Dr. Martin Luther King and today's major mega-churches and ministries of godly black men and women have changed our nation. How they could forgive white people and still love Jesus are miracles of God. But for so many it has happened, and God has blessed us in this country in spite of our ways.

Now the greatest problem blacks or any ethnic group will have to deal with is doing the same thing to others. Those of us who went through the Vietnam era had to chuckle when we read in the newspaper that with 150 language groups in Arlington, Virginia, some of the Vietnamese were upset that so many "foreigners" were moving in. It is a common, human malady that we all of us must face.

I thought once that I would be a Jew and live in Israel with my children and their children's children after us. The harsh treatment and injustice that we received from the courts devastated me. For at least two or three years, I woke up in the night sobbing, and I fought depression during the day. In time, with much prayer and meditation on God's Word, I was able to put that behind me and recover my deep love for Israel and the Jewish people.

I stand up for the Jewish people wherever I go and see our lives as unalterably linked together. But I have no expectation of being officially Jewish now and have simply returned to being an everyday follower of Jesus. I consider that the Torah, Hebrew language, the prophets and Psalms belong as much to me as to anyone. Moses is my Moses. Elijah is my Elijah. Jesus is my Jesus. I don't really need a name or title anymore.

I do hope and pray, however, that the entire world will try to move a little closer to listening and understanding each other. But this is all written after the fact, and we must continue on to our second move to Israel.

CHAPTER 9
Aliyah: Back to Israel

*A**liyah** is the Hebrew word for "going up." It refers to those immigrating to Israel with a view to becoming citizens under the Law of Return. The idea comes from the fact that Jerusalem is higher than any other place. When speaking of the City of Faith, you would never say, "Come on down." No, when you go to Jerusalem, you have to go up.

Interestingly enough, the last word of the Old Testament is II Chronicles 36:23. (the original order of the Hebrew Scriptures placed this book last). It is a proclamation by Cyrus, King of Persia, which says, *"The Lord, the God of heaven, has given me all the kingdoms of the earth and he has appointed me to build a temple for him at Jerusalem in Judah. Anyone of his people among you—may the Lord his God be with him, and let him **go up**."* That is, "go up" to Israel. Significantly, God's last word to the Jewish people, in the Hebrew Scriptures, is the command to "go up"—to return to Israel.

Equally significant is the fact that modern Israel is a nation built on the immigration of Jews throughout the world, with a **command** to leave the Diaspora and go back up to their national, ancestral and God-promised homeland. What God commanded through King Cyrus, He is fulfilling today. And it was our desire and intent to support and be a part of those who had already made Aliyah.

However, since we had not heard anything from the Office of Immigration, I asked a friend in Israel to have a lawyer look into the matter before we made a final decision to leave for Israel. The lawyer called us and told us that, up to that point in time, his investigations indicated that our applications never arrived in Israel. He further advised us that I should come to Israel and reapply. He assured me that he would accompany me through the whole procedure.

Our purpose in seeking to make Aliyah was simply to live out a Jewish lifestyle as citizens of Israel, while at the same time demonstrating that this was not inconsistent with believing in Jesus. We did not consider ourselves missionaries and we did not want others to think of us that way. We had determined, however, if we had the opportunity, we would like to establish a house synagogue where we could model what we had concluded as a result of my studies at Fuller Seminary. I was, and remain, convinced that this was typical of the first century followers of Jesus, and it was our desire to recapture that for our day. Followers of Jesus were simply a part of the Nazarene sect of Judaism (Acts 24:5).

In any case, we had come to stay. I had a job that was being provided by a Wheaton classmate; the kids would be attending Israeli Public Schools; and Patty wanted to continue her career as an artist. As much as we could, we were prepared for life in Israel, including my willingness to serve in the Miloweem (the reserve of the Israel Defense Forces). In addition, we fully expected our children to serve in the military when they came of age. This was all part of life in Israel.

Life in Israel

Upon our return to Israel, and following an open and on-going invitation, we decided to stay with friends, at least for a while, in the Tel Aviv suburb of Ramat HaSharon. It was a delightful and peaceful community and a wonderful place to bring up children. We arrived in late August 1974. In September, the kids started school in an Israeli Public School, where all the classes were taught in Hebrew.

Israel's school system is equipped to handle new immigrants who come with no knowledge of Hebrew. Basically, the plan is to throw the kids into a program of total immersion in Hebrew, where they either sink or swim. And wonder of wonders, they all swim, some better than others, but they all seem to make it. Our daughter Rachel entered the first grade and the first language she read and wrote was Hebrew with amazing quickness.

How well I remember, after being in Israel no more than three months, hearing children yelling and arguing in Hebrew in our front yard. Thinking they were neighborhood kids, I was astonished to look out the window and see that they were our own daughters, Sarah and Rachel, arguing in fluent Hebrew. And here I was still struggling for words to find directions to the local market or locate the nearest restroom.

Patty, too, found her niche early on. As a matter of fact, the day after we arrived in Ramat HaSharon we took an evening walk though the neighborhood. During that walk we met an attractive young Israeli woman that Patty clicked with immediately. I think it was because they were both artists. In any case, this brought an instant introduction to the art world of Israel, a world that she, by God's grace, entered in an extraordinarily short time and at an extraordinarily high level.

During our stay in Israel she had the opportunity to exhibit with some of Israel's most prominent artists, as well as hold solo shows both in Israel and the United States. It was a kind of artistic heyday for her. So much was lost when we had to leave Israel. But I am getting ahead of myself.

One of our means of livelihood at that time was to serve as the marketing coordinator for a firm in the United States that made concrete handling equipment. The machinery had been invented and the company was owned and operated by a classmate of mine from Wheaton College, Bob Oury. It was a brilliant system of conveyor belts strung together to transport huge amounts of concrete over long distances. Bob was excited about having his equipment in Israel and even had visions of it being used to help build the Third Temple in Jerusalem. Bob never thought small.

My job was to contact building contractors to determine their interest in the equipment. Actually, there was limited interest because, while construction was one of Israel's major industries at that time, along with tourism, the machines we offered were used for huge building projects such as dams and air fields—projects that require enormous amounts of concrete and enormous amounts of money.

As a small country, Israel had a limited demand for this kind of machinery, but there was some potential. Part of our salary package for representing this company included a brand new Volvo station wagon for our use. This work was part of the means of livelihood for us and we also cashed in every retirement program we had, sold everything we could to raise money, and used all the money we had saved while in the military. We burned the bridges and never looked back.

Another means of support was through the Watchmen Association, the non-profit organization we had formed before leaving Wheaton for Fuller Seminary. A few friends and family stood with us in our desire to identify with Israel and the Jewish people. We kept them informed on a regular basis by letters, sharing what we were doing and how our plans to return to Israel were progressing. All were favorable to Israel and supported our desire to model the possibility of living a distinctively Jewish life while still believing in Jesus.

Those in the Watchman Association took the Bible at face value and saw that this was certainly true in Jesus' day and believed as we did that it could and should be an option. At least that is what we thought at the time about all those who were receiving our newsletter. We were deeply wounded later on, as you will see, to find there was a traitor in the camp.

Application for Citizenship

After we settled in, the time had come for us to complete the applications for becoming citizens of the State of Israel, as Jews under the Law of Return. We had filled out all the papers in California and I quote from one of the newsletters at that time:

> "Concerning our application for immigration to Israel, as you know, I submitted our applications last September (this was May). Since then, I have tried repeatedly here in the Los Angeles area office, and by writing directly to the Office of Immigration in Israel, to get some response. To date there has been absolutely no response. In April of this year, however, I asked a friend of ours to have an Israeli lawyer look into the matter. The lawyer called us this week and said that at this point, his investigation indicates that our applications never arrived in Jerusalem. At least there is no record of it. He further advised me that I should come to Israel as soon as possible, initially without the rest of the family, and reapply there. He assured me that he will accompany me through the procedure. He suggested that we should know within three to four weeks after the application is filed, the direction it is going to take. At any rate, I plan to leave for Israel on or before the 10th of June, in order to pursue the matter further. Patty and the children will remain in Pasadena until I return."

That was in May of 1974. In August of that same year, after trying to get some word, we talked with friends in Israel who encouraged us to come on to Israel and apply there, just as the lawyer had suggested in the first place. Two days before I was to leave on the trip in June to pursue the matter, I received word from the lawyer that he would be gone from Israel for four to six weeks, so there seemed to be little point in going at that time.

Basically, we just returned to what we sensed God impressed us to do from the beginning—return to Israel as a family. We believed that we would eventually be granted citizenship, but that at this point we felt we had to just step out in faith as Abraham had done. I actually thought about the fact that Abraham did not receive an invitation from Canaan before he left Ur of the Chaldees. Finally, we hired a California company to temporarily put all our household goods in ready-to-ship overseas storage cartons, until we could find a place in Israel.

After flying to Israel with a few suitcases of clothes and personal items, we rented a house and set about to get the children enrolled in school, establish a household and catch our breath after the long trip. One letter I wrote home at that time said, "In order to put 'legs' to our beliefs and to identify with the hopes and aspirations of Israel and the Jewish people, as well as to be a part of what God is doing among the Jewish people in these 'latter days,' my family and I did what we believed God wanted us to do—we became Jews."

I proceeded to inform how the organization we started was different in that it was not a "missionary" organization as some may see it, because we were not seeking "converts" or "proselytes as these terms have been used traditionally. "To convert" has meant to a Jew to stop being a Jew and become a "culturalized" Western Christian.

Becoming a "Christian" has meant an acceptance of an unwritten code that says one is no longer to identify himself as a Jew. It had meant ethnic suicide. As a "Christian," he is expected to eat pork, join a local church, worship at 11:00 a.m. on Sunday morning, etc., all of which are cultural expressions. To "become a Christian" has long ceased to mean a "follower of Messiah," as it did to first century believers in Jerusalem.

Some time after that, we finally met with the lawyer who was to help us. Our first meeting was a shocker. We were hardly ready for what took place. He showed us a copy of one of the newsletters we had mailed out in California, which had been given to him by the Ministry of the Interior. The contents of the newsletter had been one of the reasons our application was denied. Basically, because we believed in Jesus, we could not be considered Jews and thus did not qualify to immigrate under the Law of Return. Our identity as Jews was in question.

He indicated that our case would have to go to the Supreme Court to get a resolution. That was because all questions of Jewish identity automatically go to the Supreme Court, sitting as the High Court of Justice. That was certainly not what we had in mind. Obviously, someone who had access to our newsletters deliberately sent it to the Ministry of Interior in Israel. We have no idea who it was and perhaps will never know. It really doesn't matter now, but from that time on we were considered the enemy in the eyes of *some* of the religious establishment.

I want to stress that almost every single Israeli we knew supported us. Positive articles were written in the newspapers and magazines about our being in Israel. Dozens of neighbors who lived around us personally asked what they could do to help. But from the standpoint of some religious Jews and rabbis, even from the time of our discussions with the rabbi in Chicago we knew that our desire to become Jews and retain our faith in Jesus was controversial. Not only had the Chicago rabbi been hesitant, but had quietly written to Israel to an important Israeli rabbi for advice.

We came to believe, and do to this day, that it was God's sovereign will that everything happened just as it did. We can see now that while our motives were genuine, our desires sincere and our actions driven by our understanding of biblical truth, we are now in a much better position to help Israel and the Jewish people from America as Christians. It was a painful rebuke and rejection, but we have seen and are seeing Paul's glorious declaration become a reality, *"All things work together for good to those who love the Lord, to those who are called according to His purpose"* (Romans 8:26). But back to the story as it unfolded.

In addition to the problems with our newsletter, we learned for the first time from our lawyer that our conversion had been revoked. Unbelievably and unknown to us, this had actually taken place before we even left the United States. No one had made any attempt to contact us or inform us of this action by the Chicago Rabbinical Council, which would have completely altered our decisions. Thus began the difficult and uncertain days of 1974-1976. The lawyer we retained, Gad Reveh, was recommended to us as one who was familiar with the issues involved and had argued cases before the High Count of Justice on many occasions.

Regardless of his knowledge and expertise, the months dragged on and we seemed to be making very little progress. While we never lost hope and continued to believe God for His intervention, as I look back, the end was predictable. Jews who believe in Jesus are simply not considered Jews by most of the legal and rabbinical judges of Israel. Even today it all seems so surreal.

How can it be that Jesus, born and raised a Jew, whose disciples were Jewish and practiced the Judaism of the day, who had multitudes of Jewish people following Him, would not be recognized as worthy of being followed by Jews today? Of course, the huge stumbling block then to a small contingent of the religious leaders is the same today—Jesus claimed to be the Son of God. He even went so far as to say, *"Anyone who has seen me has seen the Father"* (John 14:9).

John wrote of Jesus the verse so offensive to some and so precious to others, *"For God so loved the world that he gave his one and only Son, that whoever believes in him shall not perish but have eternal life"* (John 3:16).

The Apostle Paul, a "Hebrew of the Hebrews," further explained: *"Even to this day when Moses is read, a veil covers their hearts. But whenever **anyone** turns to the Lord, the veil is taken away"* (II Corinthians 3:15). Although the day spoken of there was 2000 years ago, the prophet Zachariah foresaw another day. God declared, *"I will pour out on the house of David and the inhabitants of Jerusalem a spirit of grace and supplication. They will look to me, as the one they have pierced, and they will mourn for him as one mourns for an only child, and grieve bitterly for him as one grieves for a firstborn son. On that day a fountain will be opened to the house of David and the inhabitants of Jerusalem, to cleanse them from sin and impurity"* (Zechariah 12:10; 13:1).

To us, all these verses made sense, but throughout the whole process there was no indication that a "spirit of grace and supplication" was visited on the judges who were making the decision regarding our case. Again, as I look back, it was a foregone conclusion—we were guilty of trying to immigrate to Israel as Jews who believed in Jesus. That was totally unacceptable. We were, in the words of one judge, "vomited out." Some of our friends were not willing for that to be the last word and urged us to see another lawyer and go to the religious courts. Our hopes were dimmed, but we decided to go ahead with an appeal to the religious courts.

We contacted Amnon Zicharoni, an attorney of national reputation in Israel who also had dealt with similar issues of Jewish identity. His evaluation was basically that the High Court had the last word as far as our legal identity was concerned. However, he urged us to take it to the Rabbinical Council of Tel Aviv for a religious finding on our identity. He did not encourage us to believe the results would be any different.

Amnon Zicharoni contended that sooner or later a breakthrough would occur for people like us, but for that to happen we had to keep chipping away. We appealed to the Tel Aviv Rabbinical Council—and he was right, the result was the same—we were guilty! That was it. Our dream that had become a nightmare was ended. The hole in our hearts was still there and would remain for a long time. Shortly after we received the decision from the Rabbinical Council, we also received a letter from the Ministry of Interior, telling us our visas had expired and we had to leave the country or face fines and/or imprisonment.

I must confess I did consider the latter alternative, but only briefly. I was reading in Psalm 37:3-4, *"Trust in the Lord and do good; Dwell in the land and feed on His faithfulness. Delight yourself also in the Lord, And he shall give you the desires of your heart."* My thought was to send Patty and the children home and I would *"dwell in the land and feed on His faithfulness."*

Would He not give me the desires of my heart—to dwell in the land, if I delighted myself in Him? Maybe I would be imprisoned and perhaps the Lord could use that to somehow get a reversal to our case. It sounded right, but then so did our whole conversion experience, and look how that ended, I thought. I was not sure how straight my thinking was in the wake of all that had happened.

One thing I did know was that we, as a family, needed each other more than we ever had before. Being in prison would not help my family, and at this point, they had to come first. It was important to stay together not only in Israel, but also when we came back to the United States. As a matter of fact, I didn't realize at the time how important it would be for us to be together once we returned to America. The same rejection we experienced in Israel, we would now experience from some friends as we returned to our homeland—and that was something for which we were not prepared. But let Patty speak from her point of view.

Patty's Perspective

Today, in 2004, I rummaged through boxes of papers and information from our days in Israel. There are the conversion papers, the wedding certificate, the affidavit the Chicago lawyer made after interviewing the rabbi who converted us, the letters back and forth to and from my brother, a lawyer in New Orleans, and Gad Raveh, our lawyer in Israel.

I remember how shocked Max was when he read the lawyer's name. We called him Gad as in "god," which was his name. Max asked unbelievingly, "The man's name is God?" He always called him Gad, as in glad. Max was a very bright man and obviously knew that languages are different, but he made a big deal over some things and this was one of them. I finally explained to him that one of my buddies in the art world in Israel was called Doo-doo, a short, friendly, nickname for David, and we moved on to other issues.

I still have clippings of all the art exhibitions I was in, of articles written about us in the Jerusalem Post and other things that I put out of sight for the last thirty years. At first, I refused to take part in writing about these things. Then I said, "I'll think about it." Finally, I decided to just get over it, start writing and see where it would lead.

I think my own worst fault in this whole experience was the naïve attitude I had. I have always leaned toward thinking that if you just explain things enough, people will understand. I assumed if I didn't hurt anyone or have any ill will, everyone else would be the same. When I look at some the newsletters the office put out, I would say some things differently, but what we were doing was such a huge leap that I thought others would know that normal people don't convert to Judaism and take their kids with them unless they are honestly seeking to be a part of the life of a people.

The entire experience reminds me of the "for better or for worse" clause in the marriage vows. No one has the slightest idea what that means when they say it in a ceremony. For richer or for poorer? In sickness or in health? Till death do us part? Are you serious?

Who among us could say they have never questioned those vows a wee bit and might have hesitated a little longer if they had known the future? A time or two, I even thought about the boyfriend I left behind in Louisiana and wondered where he was and how he was doing. Not that I didn't love Jim Hutchens. Anyway, if you love God and believe in the Bible, you begin to learn more about what true love is from the Source of Love and are able to draw on His strength to make it through the trials and disappointments of life.

I can tell you that moving to Israel the second time was one of the most wonderful, fascinating and productive times of my life. It was also a huge trial and disappointment. As we went through those two years, I grieved like a pregnant woman carrying triplets, knowing she faced a long and a difficult road with no other option but to go through it.

We had no sooner arrived in Israel than we received word that our efforts to immigrate were in trouble. Not too long after that, we got the notice that the rabbi had cancelled the conversions. My first thought was a carnal one—to ask for the blood back. Trust me, our conversion may have appeared totally suspicious to some of the religious leaders, but I would not have dreamed of hauling my three beloved children across the ocean and putting them through the ordeal we went through. I look at them today and marvel at how normal they are and what wonderful, responsible adults they have become. The eleven grandchildren are just boatloads of icing on the cake.

In fact, if it had not been for our children, it would have been impossible to make it. One serious flaw I've had as long as memory serves is that of trying to please people. It even leads to what is a real sin—fear of men's faces.

Perhaps it comes from being raised in a dysfunctional home, but then Jim points out that probably all homes are somewhat dysfunctional. However, since I was the last of four children with a 15 year difference from top to bottom, and since I have the personality of my Daddy instead of my Mama, a major part of my life was spent trying to please parents, siblings, teachers, boyfriends and even strangers. It has been a heavy burden to bear, and being married to someone like me is a real trial.

My loving Daddy never said a critical word to me, and he used to say to anyone who complained about my tears, "Leave the baby alone; she's just like her Daddy: She wears her heart on her shoulders." But Daddy was gone now and others never proved as easy to please, no matter how good I tried to be.

Let's start with the first day we got off the plane at Lod Airport and strolled around in Ramat Hasharon, (high place of the Sharon) which is near Tel Aviv. From that day until the one two years later when our recently Bar-mitzvahed son had to help me and the girls get onto the plane to fly out of Israel, the everyday people of Israel were terrific.

We lived in an area populated mostly with immigrants from South Africa, although some had come from other countries in the Middle East. Our next door neighbor came to Israel with nothing, but founded and owned "Anglo-Saxon," one of the premier real estate companies in Israel. Across the street was a doctor who had invented some great innovation in the medical world. On one side was a couple who were Sephardic Jews who immigrated to Israel years ago from either Iraq or Iran.

That first day, the children learned from Yehezkiel how to say *gum* (mastic) and *enough* (maspik) in Hebrew. A day or so later, his wife Ariella cooked one of the most incredible Yemenite meals I ever ate, and we were close friends and neighbors from that day on.

We went for a walk that first day on Rehov Hamelachim (Street of the Kings) and met Magda, a beautiful Polish woman who, with her sister Anat, had survived the Holocaust by passing as daughters of a brave Catholic family there. We found that many Jews were saved in just this manner, some by being able to live openly as part of a Christian family, others by being hidden in every conceivable hide-a-way in the country.

Magda told me of an art studio in Tel Aviv where artists worked and gave me the address and phone number. As we continued to walk, we met one man who had immigrated years before and appeared to be a western type person with an American accent. We chatted a few minutes, then when he heard we planned to immigrate, he turned to us and said, "Go back. Go back. There is still time to turn back. Listen to me, do not immigrate to Israel." Of course, we laughed and pretended he was joking. He was, however, very serious.

We rented the house of a friend who was out of country and set up housekeeping. I was told that people needed work and that if we had even a small amount of money, it would be good to hire someone to help me clean. I decided to try it and hired a woman the neighbor suggested. She did a good job—when I let her work. It lasted for a few weeks, but we decided we couldn't really afford it. Besides that, I sat much of the time with her, trying to learn Hebrew. I often prepared her lunch, sat down and ate with her and usually cleaned up beforehand so she wouldn't think I was a poor housekeeper. The wife of our neighbor was so bad at this, her husband forbade her to even talk to the housekeeper. Some folks are just destined to do their own housework.

That very week I went to the art studio in Tel Aviv. As soon as I walked in the door, Yuval Yariv, an enormously talented, bohemian type Sabra (Israeli-born), invited me to start working *that day*. I told him I didn't have a zinc plate for etching, but he pulled one out from under the table where the acids sat and offered it to me. This was a man who lived in a tiny little room on top of someone's roof and paid his rent with artwork. Yet, he gave me a piece of zinc immediately. That is how Israelies are. Generous. Talented. Friendly. Interested and interesting.

Every week I worked at least one day in the printmaking studio and began to apply some of the recently acquired skills learned from Ben Sacoguchi in California. Not long after, a well-known Israeli artist came in the studio and said, "Yael, I am supposed to be in this book with Israeli artists. It is going to be called *Isart*. You take my place. I don't want to be in it."

I asked him if it would be okay for me since I was new in town. He said, "It was my place. Now it's your place." And so it was.

Here was an instant invitation to share in a publication of artists, which was followed by more invitations to be in group shows and opportunities to spend time with fellow artists, discussing art, religion and politics. Israelies are real, open and honest—Israeli artists even more so. And these artists knew what I believed and could have cared less.

Even in Israel, occasionally someone would come up to Jim or me and whisper that they were believers in Jesus, but they could not tell anyone for fear of loss of job or some other punishment. For a person who grew up in the Bible belt in America, I had no idea what it would be like to have those worries—at least for people in my denomination. We had a dozen Bibles in the house, and prayed before meals, in school and before sporting events. Occasionally when a family would dine out and pray before the meal, the owner of the restaurant would come over and tell them the meal was free. Imagine that.

However, if you weren't in the right denomination, it would be another question. So, in a way, we had our own lack of freedoms. And if races mixed in church at that time in our history, you were in deep trouble. God willing, we are beyond those days. Although I am more confident than some about the future of faith in America, even with the upsurge of television programs, mega-churches and people talking about Jesus, is it possible that the day will come when we will not have the same access to the things we have ignored or taken for granted for years?

One thing that I found in Israel is that people we knew in our neighborhood and vicinity did not flinch over religious or political discussions of any kind. Our friends and our children's friends knew our family believed in Jesus. Yet, the rabbi at the local synagogue we attended said that Matt was his best Bar-Mitzvah student in years. He told us that Matt really believed in what he was doing and worked hard at learning his part of the Torah reading.

We kept kosher and either had people over or went to a neighbors for Shabbat dinner every week. Once someone gave us a live chicken as a gift and, just like others would have done, we took it to the shochet (ritual slaughterer) to kill it in a kosher fashion. We learned the prayers at the synagogue and slowly began to be a real part of the life of the community.

The Phantom Kid

One of the unusual things that happened to us during this time had to do with our children. Warner Fox came to Israel to make a children's western—that is, a movie about the west where all the actors are children. Mostly, they were recruiting children from ages eight to thirteen or so, with some smaller ones included in bit parts.

Matt was chosen for a major role. He played the banker who, in the end, turned out to be boss of the bank robbers. Sarah played the part as of an older woman in the film, and Rachel had a bit part as one who was riding the train when the bad guys robbed it. In her scene she was told to look frightened and come out of the train with her hands up. Every time they shot her scene, she indeed did come out with her hands up. And every time, she not only looked frightened. She was frightened. As a matter of fact, she cried real tears at every retake. We kept telling her it was just pretend, but she never really got it.

This film, **The Phantom Kid,** took weeks to film, and I accompanied our children whenever they had to be in a shooting. The producer and most of the others working on the film became good friends before it was over. When the still photographer quit and left the country over some squabble, I volunteered to shoot the stills. I was then asked to paint a poster that would be printed and distributed all over Israel on the kiosks. I could see quite readily how directing and shooting films could become a passion.

Later, Yankele HaMeiri, the producer of this film and a good friend who had welcomed me as if I'd lived in Israel all my life, was killed in a car wreak en route to Jerusalem. It was a painful experience to stand with his wife, family and friends and watch this healthy, talented man's life vanish as he was dropped into the ground, wrapped in a sheet. I couldn't help but think about Lazarus and wish that Jesus would show up.

Ayin Bayah

Like most of our former life, we didn't have an excess of money. Finally, one day when we really were low in the back account, I went to the grocer who had a little store around the corner from our house. I told him we were short of money and had heard that some people had accounts with him. He was so cheerful and non-condescending.

He enthusiastically told me, "Ayin bayah. (There's no problem here). Just buy anything you want anytime and I will put it on your bill. Someday, when you have the money, you can pay me."

I asked him if the children could come in before or after school and get yogurt or something and would he also include them on the bill?

"Ayin bayah," he assured me as he got out a little sheet of paper to set up an account. "In fact, you can wait a year or two if you want to—or even later."

Because inflation was so bad at that time, everyone knew that it might actually help merchants to get the money months later. One day we woke up to the news that the money was worth one-fourth less than what it had been the day before. People actually invested in extra washing machines and other appliances so that they could sell them later for more money. Imagine having a dollar bill drop in value to eighty cents overnight. Then, a few weeks later, see it go to fifty cents. There were so many devaluations in the years we were there; it was easy to see how desperate people could become. We were grateful to have what money we had in dollars in the bank, so it never devalued. At any rate, it worked well for us and for him and we were grateful.

Miracle House

After a year, the friend, whose home we had rented, came back. We had to find another place. We knew of an empty house around the corner on Rehov Yegia Capaim (Street of work of the hands). We inquired about the owner and Jim called him. He happened to be an American Jew who was married to an Israeli and spent much of the time out of the country. When Jim called him to rent the house, he said, "No, I don't want to rent the house."

Later, Jim called him again and pressed, telling him that we lived in the area and were in real need of a place for the family. Again, he said, "No." But Jim and I and children continued to walk by the house. We began to sense that God wanted us to live in that house and that we had to call him again. Vines were growing out the windows and it was in total disarray inside and out. We were sure he would change his mind.

"Eli, it's Jim again," Jim said somewhat sheepishly when he called him. "Could you just reconsider renting your house? We haven't been able to find anything else near the school."

"Hutchens, I told you no, and I mean no. DO NOT CALL ME AGAIN."

Jim turned and said that Eli told him not to call him again. We knew we had a serious problem on our hands. So we began to fast and pray for several days. We enlisted a few friends to join us in crying out to the Lord to help us with this need. We asked God to change Eli's heart and cause him to let us rent the house. We reminded the Lord of the verse: *"The king's heart is in the hand of the Lord. He moved it which ever way He chooses"* (Proverbs 21:1).

However, Jim reminded me that Eli had told him not to call him again. So we prayed and thought about it another day or two. Then it occurred to me.

"Jim, he did not tell *me* not to call. Give me his number. I will call him."

I called Eli and said, "Eli, it's Yael Hutchens. The reason you are not renting the house to us is because you do not know our story. Would you come over and just hear us out?" I could hear his wife in the background saying something.

"Oh, I guess so, if for nothing else, to get you guys out of my face," he finished.

So, we set up a time right away and he and his wife came to the house and we had dinner and talked during the evening. We told him how we had converted to Judaism and still retained our belief in Jesus and how we were having some trouble with immigration and had to go to court. His wife immediately turned to him and said, "See Eli, I told you that you should rent the house to them."

So Eli agreed to rent us the house. Then Jim said, "Eli, we have been praying about this for some time and we asked the Lord how much money we should pay each month."

Eli regained that exasperated look he had earlier, and said, "And how much did God tell you to pay me?" He had been asking $350 a month.

Jim said, "$250."

His wife leaned over, nearly punched him and said, "I told you, Eli." So Eli rented us the house for the amount of money the Lord had told us to pay, and we began a deep and abiding friendship. That was the house where we either went to other homes or invited friends in the neighborhood for weekly kosher Shabbat dinners - or just coffee and cake. That was the house where we studied Hebrew for hours. That was the house next door to the empty lot where the kids built bon fires and ate pistachio nuts and listened to classical music. That was the house one block in one direction from the school and one block in the other from the little corner store. That was the house where many children and some adults slept in sleeping bags the night before we had to leave Israel. That was the house where we spent our last night.

That was the house where huge chunks of our hearts were left behind.

CHAPTER 10
The Agony of Defeat:
Residuals from Rejection

Defeat always has collateral damage. The mere fact that we had to return to the United States was a clear statement of defeat. Being kicked out of Israel because of what we believed was defeat. Somehow we felt like lepers—unclean because of the failure of our faith. Or, rather than faith, had it been presumption?

I asked myself, "Had we willingly placed ourselves in a position where it would have taken a miracle from God for us to survive?" If so, that's what Jesus called tempting God when He was challenged by Satan to jump off the highest point of the temple. Had we tempted God? Now we had to be accountable to those who knew us and supported us from the States. How could we explain the failure of something we believed in with such passion? How would we be received? Actually, we had a preview of coming attractions before we even left Israel.

It came in an after dark visit by some friends who were Jews, but believers in Jesus as Messiah. I was reminded of the visit of Nicodemus to Jesus after dark. When we greeted them at the door, we were so delighted to see them, but no sooner had they come in than they honestly told us that they could only stay a minute. They had parked a street away and walked around the back so no one would see them coming to our house. It was risky and just like Nicodemus, they didn't want to take the chance of being seen or identified with us. They were scared.

One might question why they came, but we welcomed them and thanked them. They wanted us to know they were praying for us. That was good—we needed prayer. But we also needed acceptance and the manner of their visit left that in doubt.

On the other hand, there were numbers of Jewish and Christian friends who walked with us throughout the whole ordeal. They never wavered. They were always there when we needed them. Everyone knew the ramifications for followers of Jesus, especially Jewish believers.

Would Israel ever open her arms to them as she has to all other Jews? Or would Jews who believe in Jesus be the modern pariahs—rejected and unaccepted? The Court's decision was not encouraging. What irony in it all. One could scarcely find anyone more pro-Israel than those among the Jewish believers, both in and out of Israel. Then, as now, Israel needed all the friends she could get.

Fortunately, the tide has turned today to some degree. Many Jewish believers in Israel are responsible and productive citizens in their professions and fields of endeavor. In some cases, they are known to be Jewish followers of Jesus. They are making significant contributions to the life, health and welfare of Israel. The same is true of gentile Christians. While many remain suspicious of any Christian support because of fear that it is only a cover for evangelism, most are coming to realize that Christians, who truly believe the Bible, are the best friends Israel has.

Christian Zionists are the most active, vocal supporters Israel has—often more active and vocal than some Jews, especially liberal Jews with no biblical knowledge. We were and remain biblical Zionists, but that didn't help us when we returned from Israel. For the most part, the press pilloried us.

As a matter of fact, our case received considerable press coverage in the United States. One article in the New York Times spoke of us as "wolves in sheep's clothing." Another in the Chicago Tribune echoed those sentiments, stressing we had attempted to manipulate the system in a less than honest way. They questioned our integrity. One writer in the Los Angeles Times accused us of blatant deception—of trying to pass ourselves off as something we were not.

The secular press can be distressing, but some Christian publications hyped our case when they jumped on the bandwagon. Too many Christians even bought into the myth that a person could not be a Jew and believe in Jesus. One had to wonder what New Testament they were reading. One pastor showed his true colors when he demanded a statement of public repentance on our part for attempting to identify with a godless, works-oriented, blasphemous religion like Judaism. In those days, it was "damned if you did" and "damned if you didn't."

Even some of our close friends changed their views of us based largely on the secular press. One couple, former Wheaton classmates, questioned the terminology we used. In Israel we spoke of Jesus by His Hebrew name -Yeshua. Some found that very disturbing—that we did not refer to Jesus with the English word for Jesus, but used a "foreign" name for Jesus. They said we compromised our faith by using Yeshua instead of Jesus and wrote that we were ashamed of the name of Jesus. It reminds me of those who never question whether the King James Version of the Bible was the first version. It takes time for long held views to be altered.

I wanted those who knew and trusted us to hear from me personally. With that in mind, I went back to Dallas Seminary and requested and appointment with Dr. John Walvoord, the President of the Seminary, and a man for whom I had great respect. We spent an hour together, while

I recounted for him the whole conversion process and our attempt to immigrate to Israel under the Law of Return—how that was rejected resulting in our return to the States. I will never forget his response.

Dr. Walvoord said, "Jim, it's obvious that you have a great love for Israel and the Jewish people. I admire you for that - for your willingness and desire to identify so fully with them."

He said, "But you must remember, as a believer in Christ, you can never go from the Church and become Israel." At that point I realized that his Dispensational Theology, with its strict distinction between Israel and the Church, would preclude any acceptance of what we had attempted to do.

The fact that Gentile believers in Jesus have been "grafted in" to the root of Israel (Romans 11:17) does not fit well with a strict Dispensational paradigm. To think that we could personally be a part of the "Israel of God" (Galatians 6:16) in a literal way was to think too far outside the box. It was pointless to pursue it, even with this good friend and respected mentor.

However, I did pursue the issue by returning to the Fuller Theological Seminary. One of my most pleasant recollections occurred there. I arrived mid-morning the day I returned to the campus. Just after chapel, many of the students and faculty had gone to the Student Center for coffee and donuts. As I walked in, the first person my eyes connected with was the Dean of the School of Theology, Dr. Glenn W. Barker.

Seeing me, he immediately came to me and said, "Jim we've followed your pilgrimage with much interest and prayers. You and your family took a bold and courageous course into uncharted waters, and I just want you to know how proud we are of you." He went on, "I know how disappointing the outcome must be for you and your wife, but I want you to know how much we appreciate your efforts—I want you to know we're for you."

Those positive words from someone like Dr. Barker came like rain on a parched desert. He has since gone on to be with the Lord, but Patty and I will never forget Dr. Glenn W. Barker, a friend who *"stuck closer than a brother."*

Dr. Arthur F. Glasser was also such a friend. He had been my mentor for my doctoral studies and dissertation. He was also a great encouragement. Seeing him and his dear wife Alice was nothing short of a healing. His great love for Israel and the Jewish people had knit us together during my studies, and that relationship was only reinforced when I returned, even in defeat. His insight served to remind us that the history of the Jews in the Old Testament is a chronicle of God himself often being spurned and rejected by those He loved and wanted to bless. And then there is Jesus. While the multitudes followed Him, some of the religious decision makers saw Him as a threat and wanted no part of Him. Indeed, times have not changed much.

Nicholas Worth was a friend from the day we met him. Jewish to the core, he was an incredibly talented Hollywood actor with whom we served in the 101st Airborne Brigade in Fort Campbell, Kentucky. Nicholas strongly felt led to enlist in the Army and serve his country. When we came to Fort Campbell, he was one of the first people we met. Within minutes after Patty met him, she asked him to present a program on Shakespeare to the Women's Club.

Nicholas was and is like a brother to us both. He followed us through our entire trek in Israel and beyond. When we returned, he called and asked, "James, do you want me to go to Israel and 'take names and kick butt?'" This hulk of a man was a mighty power lifter and could have definitely carried out the threat, but we laughed and simply requested, "Nicholas, pray for us."

Time has a healing effect. Some things only time can heal. We knew all the promises of God regarding Israel and believed them. Yet, the stark reality and pain of rejection would take time to produce a proper perspective. And over time it began to emerge. God seemed to be saying to us, "Your faith was not lacking—this was part of my plan—your time is yet to come."

I began to think in terms of God's timing. Was it His timing we missed? Humanly speaking, maybe so. But from God's viewpoint, no. Looking back, I believe God was saying, "It's not over, but I want you to wait—wait and you will see." It was a long wait—over twenty years, but a time of waiting during which God brought a growing maturity to my understanding of Israel. It was a time when our understanding of how we were to relate to Israel and the Jewish people would take a new and unexpected turn.

Initially, that turn came in a call from a seminary classmate to come to Washington, DC and the northern Virginia area and pastor a newly planted church. A group of *Campus Crusade for Christ* members' ministry on Capitol Hill had seen many members of Congress and their staffs come to faith in Jesus. Now they wanted to start a church where these new converts could be discipled in their faith. The call to pastor that congregation convinced me that our plans for Israel would be on hold. But before Virginia, you'll want to hear from Patty.

Patty's Perspective

Somewhere, because I'm a saver, I have the stubs of the airplane tickets from that trip back home. I have a few stones from the David/Goliath arena in Israel. I have all the documents for everything from school records to driver's licenses to Israeli medical cards. Among the records is a personal drawing and note from Manashe Kadishman, one of the world's leading artists.

I have etchings from Israeli artists with whom I traded works. I have a half-handful of little tiles from the area around Herod's temple which we got before it was illegal and cordoned off. I have fake ancient coins we bought in Israel when a man came out from behind an old building and beckoned me to look at them. I fell for it hook, line and sinker and gave him cash for "ancient silver coins." Later a knowledgeable friend laughed as he approached from the other side of the room to see them. "They are ancient all right," he said, "They are at least 48 hours old." However, he told us to keep them because fakes become collector's items.

When we show them, we say, "These are *fake, ancient,* collector coins." Sounds impressive. Maybe one day they will be worth something—in about the year 10,000 A.D.

Back to the Windy City

When we arrived in Chicago, we had nowhere to go and very little money. The children and I stayed with friends for a few days while I feverishly searched for a house to rent. The only one we found in the general area of Jim's office was in Highwood, Illinois, and the owner wanted $900 a month. Jim was still in Israel trying to sell the Volvo, so I thought, and we would soon have $6,000.

When I told the owner we would like to rent the house, he wanted references. We could get references; what we needed was money. He also wanted two months' rent in advance. In the end, he took just one month's rent and a signed note from a friend who promised to pay if we could not. I knew this was not biblical, but our friend said he really would pay for it and since he had ample finances, we knew he wasn't worried. If people earned points in heaven for good deeds, our friend Bob got some for his kindness toward us.

The night Jim called to inform me he had given the car away was a spiritual experience. My children sat there in horror as they saw their mother weeping yet again, and when it was over, I simply told them, "Daddy gave the car away." They knew we were counting on that money, but the girls hugged me and said, "Don't worry Mom; it'll be okay."

Matt thought a moment and said, "Mom, $6,000.00 is about a nickel to God." That night as I looked at our incredible children, I knew we had more treasures right there in the room than were in all the vaults of Ft. Knox. After that, with the loving, believing support of the children, the Lord seemed to lift my heart and give faith for the days ahead. Doesn't the Bible say, "A little children will lead them?"

In the fall, the kids enrolled in school and adjusted well to being back in the USA. In fact, they had adjusted well to all the moves we made. They just seemed to rise to the top, like butter on churned milk. Rachel was entering third grade, not knowing how to read or write English. The Highland Park school system had many Jewish teachers and they cheerfully took this little Hebrew-speaking child under their wings. With tutors and loving care, she was brought up to her grade level, covering four years' schooling in the next two. Jill, the grown daughter of our best friends since college, Orley and Donna Herron, took Rachel shopping at exclusive shops on the North Shore of Chicago and bought her an entire, upscale wardrobe for school.

Sarah entered junior high school and within two weeks was chosen for a special award. In no time, she knew half the town and most of the junior and senior high school. She never even skipped a beat. Matt made straight A's from the start in one of the best high schools in America and found Jay Katz, a best friend, right across the street. I started taking art lessons at The Art Institute of Chicago, my old stomping grounds.

When Jim returned from Israel, we not only didn't have the Volvo, we didn't have a car at all. But within weeks, we had six cars donated for our use. Some were sold for cash. One of them was an old VW that we later donated to the high school for auto shop classes. One was firebombed by a religious fanatic who had heard about us. I was dashing out to the car to try to put out whatever the man threw into the back seat, but Matt restrained me and said, "Mom, you can't go near it. It might blow up." Sure enough, it did. Then he continued, "Besides, Mom, we have several other cars."

After a semester at the Art Institute of Chicago, I applied for graduate school. I was rejected straight out. Friends there told me it was probably because I was older, was in no special category and had no challenged area. If they only knew how challenged I was, I thought. I was aware, however, that I had an outstanding portfolio of etchings. When I got the letter that I was not accepted, I put on blue jeans and a tee shirt, and drove to the Art Institute to get my portfolio. I later called a friend on the board, who wrote to the head of the school, who later encouraged me to reapply.

Good News from Northwestern

However, the same day I picked up the portfolio, I decided on the "spur of the moment" to go by Northwestern University on the way home. I almost stalked into the art department and told the receptionist that I had an appointment with the head of the department. Almost without looking up, she pointed to his office. When I entered Jack Burnham's office, I was angry. How what happened came about I do not know, except it was part of my destiny. He looked up from the papers on his desk and almost in a gruff way asked, "Can I help you?"

"Yes, I am interested in the Master of Fine Arts program here at Northwestern. I've just returned from two years in Israel and I have here a very good portfolio of etchings that I would like you to see." He glanced up at me and gestured for me to bring them closer as I opened up my portfolio.

I would later find out that Jack Burnham was the kind of person who gives very little approval to anybody for anything. So when he looked up at me and said, "These are very good," that was like the Hallelujah Chorus. He asked me if I spoke Hebrew and I said, "Ken . . . I mean, 'Yes.'" Then he turned in a rather abrupt way and asked, "How old are you?"

I was in no mood for foolishness, especially after the Art Institute of Chicago ordeal. Also, I was feeling personally vulnerable, because I had just turned *"40."* That sounded ancient. I told Jack, "I cannot imagine why you would ask me my age. I thought that was illegal."

In his typical unmoved-mover personality, he said, "I have to know."

I assumed that's all he meant, so I said, "Forty."

Jack then told me, "I was just this moment reading a notice. I've been notified to select a candidate for a full grant, including a stipend for living expenses, a studio and a teaching assistant slot with me." He paused, "There are two stipulations, however."

"What are the stipulations?" I asked, wondering if it had to be someone young and short.

"It has to be a female who is 40," he told me as I stood there, trying to appear calm. "When could you start?"

So began one of the most informative, energizing, productive and creative experiences of my life. As I drove home in shock, I marveled at the grace of God in a time of deep need. I took it as a sure sign that God still loved me. I remembered how Moses had been surrounded on all sides when God miraculously opened up a dry floor in the middle of seawaters. So began a to-die-for, professional relationship and an abiding, deep friendship that would change the whole direction of my life.

Right in the middle of those three years at Northwestern with Jack Burnham and Ed Paschke, both world class artists, Jim got a call from Maryland to pastor a congregation. For the first time in my life, I knew I could not go. I knew I would not go. I knew God didn't want me to go. I simply said, "I can't go, honey. If you feel you have to go, go with my blessing."

But he settled in until I finished my MFA and Matt finished high school. He even became a kind of "Mr. Mom" during those days in a noble effort to help me get my degree. The Watchmen Association, the organization we started, had grown in staff since its beginnings. That staff had been loyal to us all the time we were in Israel, but losing the court case began a slow change and eventual turning point.

It was bad enough to be rejected in Israel. Soon the group rejected us, because now they didn't think of us as Jews either. It didn't matter that any Jews who openly believed in Jesus were rejected. In time, they chose to go their way, Jim was called to start a church in Virginia and we would call ourselves "Christians" again.

Lingering Reminiscences

During those years in Illinois, Israel and all that it meant were relegated to mostly the papers, letters, stubs, pictures, crumbling newspaper articles, handwritten notes and drawers full of pictures and slides we took. For years, I hid them in boxes inside of file drawers in the farthest corner of the basement. I assumed they would not be opened until we died and the children went through our possessions.

After about two years, I quit waking up in the night sobbing. Jim and I both had tears when the children returned to dreaming in English. After about ten to fifteen years, if I quit reading the newspapers, I could go for a week or so and not even think about Israel—that is, if I also quit watching television and reading my Hebrew Bible. It was definitely like my Daddy's bacon and eggs philosophy.

Every year or so, though, I would pull out the papers and articles and glance over them. It was always when I was alone and Jim was gone. Twice, in the dead of winter, I built a blazing hot fire in our Vermont Casting wood-burning stove, gathered everything I could find together and hauled it into the family room to burn it all up. Then I would glance at a letter someone had written. Many friends wrote us before and after leaving Israel, but one treasured letter came almost immediately after the trial:

Dear Yael Hutchens,

Reading today your letter in the Jerusalem Post, I can just imagine the kind of hate mail you will receive as a result and that is one of the reasons I want to write to you so as to make sure all the letters won't be the same. Another reason is that your letter moved me and I can somewhat imagine how difficult your situation is.

I wish with all my heart that this country will feel finally secure enough to learn tolerant acceptance of various forms of thoughts. It is only a deep sign of fear and insecurity to be so rigid, to be terrified of anyone's "different" beliefs—people who are "different" in a nation, bring to this nation an enrichment, like flowers of different colors in a field.

I am certain that a time will come when all kinds of Jews and Israelis will be able to live in this country in complete freedom of thoughts, in a democratic state—white "traditional" Jews and Black Jews and Converts to Judaism and Christian Jews and Arab Jews and Messianic Jews, Reform Jews, Orthodox Jews—this day will come when peace on all fronts will come and no one will "vomit' anyone—vomiting is only a sign of sickness.

So be well and be strong. Maybe only a small group of people will stand with you, but there are such people here, too. Cordially, T.L.

Can anyone understand how much a kind letter means unless they have been in a similar situation? I read for the hundredth time newspaper articles about us. I reread the affidavits the lawyer wrote when the rabbi admitted he knew of our belief in Jesus. I remembered my brother Max in New Orleans, who had advised me to get this Chicago lawyer. I read the clippings about art exhibitions my friends and I shared and the article entitled *Haim Tegaresh Yael? (Will they drive out Yael?)*

I always recalled how I had gone to the dictionary to find out what *tegaresh* meant. It means *to drive out, to cast* or *toss out, to divorce.* I had checked the concordance to find that Adam had been *garash*ed from Eden (Gen. 3:24). Cain had been *garash*ed from the face of the earth (Gen. 4:14). Almost every time, chills would run up my spine. I usually closed off these two-to-three hour reminiscences by going over photos of friends we loved. Then I would carefully, almost religiously, fold each thing and pack all of it into the boxes, return the boxes to the basement, and return myself to the present.

We continued to learn better to live by faith, listening to tapes and memorizing Scriptures. We signed up for a Faith Conference in the south side of Chicago. The morning we were to go was the "Blizzard of 79," one of the worst in 100 years. We got up, saw the piles of snow already on the ground, looked at each other, and then agreed that snow should not keep us from a conference on faith.

As we soaked up spiritual teaching inside, we watched the snow pile up outside. When the conference ended, we realized we would have to apply what we had just learned. With difficulty, we finally got to the Dan Ryan Highway and slowly drove several miles in a blinding snowstorm toward the exit to Highland Park.

About fifty yards from the turnoff, the car abruptly stopped as we drove up on a huge snow bank in the middle of the highway. The only thing visible under the hood was snow and the motor wouldn't budge. After waiting for some time in freezing weather, Jim flagged down a man in a tow truck who promised to tow us home. He jacked the car up with us in it and slowly began to move. But at the intersection, he turned the wrong way. Watching helplessly from a steep angle, he drove us several miles in the opposite direction to his service station.

Naturally, we got out and asked why on earth he towed us further away. He said he decided it was too dangerous. Even after much pleading, he would not take us home, so, Jim said, "Matt, open up the hood. Girls, get in the car. We're going home." When I gave him a questioning look, he said, "Mom, get in the car!"

The tow truck man yelled at us as we walked toward the car, "You can't do that, mister! This is a terrible storm. You'll lose half your children!"

Matt, standing with the hood open, put his hand up with three fingers and calculated, "Half of three? Sir, that's not possible." So with the girls huddled inside, Jim and Matt put their hands on the motor and prayed a powerful, faith-filled prayer. "Turn it on, Patty," he called out to me like Jesus commanding Lazarus to come forth. I turned the key and the motor started.

We drove home high as kites, seeing what we had learned about faith working big time for us that night. Driving past the train tracks from the east side to Highland Park, we saw the lights of a train far too close for comfort. Jim never took his foot off the accelerator and we went on through, praising God all the way to the door of our barely visible house, where the car died again and was completely covered by morning. In this faith frame of mind, we eventually moved to Virginia. For me personally, heart wrenching trials were yet to come.

CHAPTER 11
Home Again:
Carry Me Back to Old Virginny

Patty is big on genealogies. She has cultivated that interest throughout our marriage. It's amazing what's back there. We both have our share of nobility and aristocracy—but also scoundrels and outlaws. I have ancestors who came over on the Mayflower. She is somehow related to Brigadier General Hugh Mercer, Chief of Staff of General George Washington, who was killed at the battle of Trenton, New Jersey. And on it goes.

My genealogy goes back to Nicholas Hutchens who was given a land grant of 264 acres in 1703 on the James River just south of Richmond, Virginia. We have fairly well determined that he was either expelled or fled from Scotland/England. Sent to Barbados, he served three years in the militia, for which he was rewarded with the land grant. Patty traced one of her mother's lines back to William Cantrell, who came to Jamestown, Virginia in 1607 and was present at the wedding of Pocahontas and John Rolfe.

So in returning to Virginia, we were in fact returning to our ancestral roots. We have often commented how much at home the whole family has felt living in Virginia. As a matter of fact, we're all here today—to date, three married children and eleven grand children. None farther than an hour and a half away and most just fifteen minutes from our home.

The church I was to pastor was an independent church and, like so many of those kinds of churches, found itself reinventing the wheel at every turn. I didn't know it at the time I came, but the leadership of the new church was committed to a concept they called "Multiple Leadership." In my view, it was a flawed leadership model from the start because each elder was considered a pastor and each pastor inevitably developed his own constituency. It became divisive.

We left after two years and the church itself shut down after about six or seven years.

Actually, for us it turned out well. We had several years of stability and productive ministry. We had been meeting with two Bible studies, both in the homes of Congressmen who had come to faith, one at the southern end and the other at the northern end of Fairfax County in Northern Virginia. The consensus of both groups was to join together in the middle, in Arlington, and plant a new church. Since I was then ordained in the Presbyterian Church in America, we decided to affiliate with that denomination.

Christ Church of Arlington had its first worship service on November 21, 1982 with thirty something people meeting in George Mason's Law School and Convention Center. In 1987 we purchased a former Disciples of Christ church building and paid off the loan in 1999. On February 1, 2004, I stepped down as Senior Pastor after more than 21 years, to go full time with a ministry supporting Israel. More on that in the next chapter.

Atten-shut! Back to the Army

When I left active duty as a chaplain in the Army in 1969, I held the rank of Major in the Regular Army. After returning to the States from our disaster in Israel in 1976, I was assigned to an active Reserve unit, completed the necessary school requirements and came to Virginia as a Lieutenant Colonel. Shortly after arriving, I inquired about the possibilities of joining the Washington, D.C. National Guard. A chaplain's slot was open and I was sworn into the National Guard in 1981. It was a great experience.

At that time, about 55 percent of the officer ranks and nearly 90 percent of the enlisted ranks in the D.C. National Guard were African American. Indeed, in some ways it was like another cross-cultural experience – one for which our experience in Israel had prepared me. But regardless of the culture or race, all people respond to love and a sense of genuine caring. The rest is just trappings. All too often those trappings are allowed to become dogma. The inevitable result is to divide and isolate. However, that was not true in the D.C. National Guard.

Our worship services served as a good example. I was usually the token white in a congregation of blacks. I always had one of the congregants led the worship and praise to include the music and the singing. It was "gospel" and it was "soul." As a matter of fact, they did all but the preaching— that was my job. And when it was my turn, I found myself spurred on and encouraged by the ever present verbal responses, "Yes," "Amen" and "Go ahead now!" of my military congregation. It was great fun and it was feedback I could rarely get from my Presbyterian congregation. After all, don't they say we Presbyterians were God's "frozen chosen."

I was soon promoted to Colonel. In 1988, I was encouraged to apply for the position of the National Guard Special Assistant to the Chief of Army Chaplains with the rank of Brigadier General. I was honored to be selected for that position, and worked mainly out of the Pentagon from 1989 to 1992 when I retired.

During Operation Desert Shield/Storm I was working out of the Pentagon. The Chief of Chaplains had me visit all the debarkation installations just to check on morale of troops and chaplains—to note the problems involved with things like family separations and dependent provision.

Encouragement was needed almost at every level.

Remember, we were expecting thousands of body bags as a result of Saddam Hussein's unleashing his chemical arsenal. One on my tasks was to assist in organizing a vast cadre from all across the country of civilian chaplains who would assist in military funerals. If that had happened—if we had 10,000 KIAs, as some were predicting, there would have been no way military chaplains alone could have handled all those funerals. We would have been swamped, literally.

By God's grace, it never happened. As a matter of fact, General Norman Schwarzkopf freely admitted the victory was miraculous. With over 500,000 in the theater, fewer than 200 of our troops were killed, and anyone who's been in a war knows that was a sign of Divine intervention. For some, this was no surprise. I'll tell you why.

Often during the Gulf War, I would go into the bowels of the Pentagon and get on a secure telephone line to Riyadh, where we made our headquarters in Saudi Arabia. I talked to the Senior Army Chaplain on General Schwarzkopf's staff, Chaplain (Colonel) David Peterson. I knew him well, since he was a member of my own denomination. I would call him just to get an in-progress report that I could pass on to the Chief of Chaplains. His reports were always upbeat.

Record numbers of worship services and Bible studies were being conducted. Baptisms based on new confessions of faith in Christ were taking place almost daily. There were probably more Bibles distributed per square foot than any place else on the planet. I remember asking him, "Dave, how do you account for this pervasive interest in spiritual things on the part of the troops?" Quickly he replied, "Because of the faithful prayers of God's people."

I knew that to be the case. Certainly, there was more prayer support sought and given throughout the United States than we ever received during Vietnam days. As a matter of fact, we started a regular prayer session in our church at that time that continues to this day. While it focused on the Gulf War then, it continues to have a strong intercessory ministry on behalf of our military.

One morning about 4:30 a.m. our phone rang. Who could this be at this hour of the morning? I picked up the phone—it was Dave Peterson calling from Riyadh. "I hope I didn't wake you, Jim."

"Oh no" I assured him, "I had to get up anyway to answer the phone." He let that pass.

"Jim, what do you know about Babylon in end-times prophecy?" he asked.

It was a little early for this. "Do you have something specific in mind?" I stalled.

"Well" he said, "General Schwarzkopf received a letter from some woman who told him he was going to be the one to fulfill end times prophecy by destroying Babylon, which is, as you know, modern Iraq. In any case, the General got a little spooked by it, because the destruction of Iraq is not part of our mission. Anyway, he gave me a direct order, 'Look into this and get back to me!'"

"Well, let me look into it, Dave, and I'll fax you what I find," I promised.

"Can I hear from you in the next 24 hours? I need to get back to the "ole man" on this one ASAP!"

"Not to worry, I'll get right on it. But if he sacks you, I want you to promise me, you'll recommend me as your replacement." I was in a good bargaining position. Besides, I was chafing under the fact that I was traveling all over the United State, trying to ratchet up the morale of chaplains and troops. At the same time my own morale needed a shot, because I wanted to be over there with the troops myself and couldn't because of stateside duties.

"Nice guy!" Dave shot back. "I'm really encouraged to know you have such a caring concern for my future. Just get the information, will you?"

"All right already—help is on the way. God Bless!" I hung up.

There's no way to go back to sleep at a time like that, so I got up and went to my study. The pertinent passages were Isaiah 13 and Jeremiah 50-51. However, as I studied these and looked at the commentaries I had, what was going on in Iraq during Desert Shield/Storm did not appear to me to be their fulfillment. These passages referred to a total devastation with no hope of restoration. And there were other events cited in these passages that seemed to clearly indicate a time still in the future.

So I put down my findings and faxed them off to Dave with the added assurance, "Tell the Boss that he is not the one—he's too early on the scene—he's off the hook. What the Bible is talking about takes place later."

As I write this, we have just had the first anniversary of our second invasion of Iraq in March 2003. When compared to the first, this one actually has more of the earmarks of fulfilled prophecy. But even here, the total devastation spoken of by the prophets has not taken place. Still, the military dimension of biblical prophecy continues to intrigue me.

Ever since I became a follower of Christ as an enlisted man through the ministry of my regimental chaplain, Burt Hatch, the Army had been a vital part of my life. Returning to the Army as a chaplain through Vietnam and then serving in the Pentagon as the Assistant Chief during the Gulf War were privileges I never expected.

Promotion to Brigadier General was both humbling and a great honor from God. Patty and I both felt deeply thankful and blessed after our failure and defeat in Israel. Dismissal from the church we had come to pastor in Virginia only added fuel to the fires of hurt and disappointment. But then, as only God can do, He lifted our spirits in a huge way. Now God seemed to be saying, "I haven't forgotten you—I am still the God of blessing and I am going to give you an unexpected blessing." The promotion was like icing on the cake of a long and wonderful military career. Gratitude fills our hearts to this day.

Awakening

During this time, like a sleeping giant, Israel was reawakening in our spirits. Aroused initially by the increased terrorism in the land, we could see the goal of the Palestinians was the ethnic cleansing of all Jews from Israel.

At first, like most of us, we considered the Middle East conflict more in political terms.

- Should not all peoples have the right to self-determination?
- Should not an evenhanded justice prevail in this dispute?
- Didn't the Palestinians have as much right to the land as the Jews?
- Had they not been uprooted from their homes in 1948 and forced into refugee status as the Jews had been so long ago?

But there was something wrong with this picture. Scripture simply did not support it.

Unlike the United States, it is impossible to separate religion and state in Israel. More correctly, it is impossible to consider the modern state of Israel apart from what God has said about it in His Word. Once you try to make that separation, the debate degenerates into a series of mutually exclusive and impossibly polarized political standoff.

God must be allowed to have the last word. And that, I would submit, is the forgotten factor in the diplomacy of the Middle East today. God does not have a seat at the table. And until He does, chaos, mass murder and mayhem will continue. But what would God bring to the table?

His Word brings clarity. *"The entrance of your words gives light; it gives understanding to the simple"* (Psalm 119:130). Certainly it is too much to expect (this side of the coming of the Messiah) for negotiators and diplomats to sit down, Bibles in hand, and work toward solutions. But it is not too much to expect those in the Judeo-Christian tradition, those who know the Bible (or who are being advised accordingly), to negotiate from biblical base. They should know, for example, what God has said about the land.

> *"On that day the LORD made a covenant with Abram and said, "To your descendants I give this land, from the river of Egypt to the great river, the Euphrates—I will establish my covenant as an everlasting covenant between me and you and your descendants after you for the generations to come, to be your God and the God of your descendants after you. The whole land of Canaan, where you are now an alien, I will give as an everlasting possession to you and your descendants after you; and I will be their God"* (Genesis 15:18, 17:7-8).

God's Word is non-negotiable. His covenants are everlasting. That means they are relevant today. Attempting to negotiate without, or apart from, this knowledge is sheer folly. It is an exercise in futility. Therefore, the Christian and Jewish communities must lobby the United States government with increased fervency and urgency regarding what God says about Israel. That these truths become bedrock in the doctrinal database of Christians and Jews is absolutely essential. All else is merely erecting speed bumps to slow down the inevitable—cultural clashes based on the notion

that we are dealing with moral and spiritual equivalents.
Palestinians and Jews are not moral and spiritual equivalents with respect to the land promised by God. God says regarding that plot of real estate, *"The land is mine!"*
(Leviticus 25:23). He further declares His authority over the land when He says the Jews are His *"tenants."*
Palestinians may warrant a state of their own for self determination purposes, but it is not foreseen by God to be within the boundaries He promised to the descendants of Abraham through Isaac and Jacob.

As a matter of fact and public record, the notion of a distinct Palestinian people was a public relations creation of Yasser Arafat after the 1967 war. The myth of a Palestinian people with their own culture, language and religion is just that—a myth. These are Arab Muslims who speak Arabic just like the Arab nations that surround them. Prior to 1948, when Israel declared independence, the people most closely identified with Palestine were Jews. Even the name "Palestine" is a Latin form of "Philistine," imposed on the land by the Romans to humiliate and demean the Jews.

However, even if one wants to argue for the legal legitimacy of a Palestinian State within present Israel, there is ample evidence to show the fallacy of that position. In a largely unknown and certainly untold story, Howard Grief spells out Israel's legitimacy in his critically important ACPR Policy Paper No. 147, "LEGAL RIGHTS AND TITLE OF SOVEREIGNTY OF THE JEWISH PEOPLE TO THE LAND OF ISRAEL AND PALESTINE UNDER INTERNATIONAL LAW." The following is an extended quote from the Executive Summary of his paper.

"These rights were recognized as inhering in the Jewish people when the highest representatives of the Great Powers that had defeated Germany and Turkey in World War I

met at the Paris and San Remo Peace Con-
ferences in 1919 and 1920. Their purpose was
to design a global political and legal settle-
ment to dispose of the conquered territories
that formerly belonged to the dissolved German and Turkish Empires. Under this settle-
ment, the whole of Palestine on both sides of
the Jordan was reserved exclusively for the
Jewish people as the Jewish National Home,
in recognition of their historical connection
with that country, dating from the Patriarchal
Period. Its boundaries were to be delineated in
accordance with the historical and biblical for-
mula "from Dan to Beersheba" which denoted
the entire Land of Israel. The Arabs were
accorded national rights in Syria, Meso-
potamia and Arabia, but not in Palestine. The
British Government as Mandatory, Trustee
and Tutor was charged with the obligation to
create an eventual independent Jewish state in
Palestine, and for this purpose only it could
exercise the attributes of sovereignty vested in
the Jewish people.

"The Palestine aspect of the global settle-
ment was recorded in three basic documents
that led to the founding of the modern State
of Israel; the San Remo Resolution of April
25, 1920, combining the Balfour Declaration
with the general provisions of Article 22 of
the Covenant of the League of Nations: the
Mandate of Palestine confirmed on July 24,
1922 and the Franco-British Boundary
Convention of December 23, 1920, supple-
mented by the Anglo-American Convention
of December 3, 1924 respecting the Mandate

of Palestine.

"The British Government repudiated the solemn obligation it undertook to develop Palestine gradually into an independent Jewish state. This began with the Churchill White Paper of June 3, 1922, and culminated with the MacDonald White Paper of May 17, 1939. The US aided and abetted the British betrayal of the Jewish people by its abject failure to act decisively against the 1939 White Paper despite its own legal obligation to do so under the 1924 treaty. The UN Partition Resolution of November 29, 1947 illegally recommended the restriction of Jewish legal rights to a truncated part of Palestine. Astonishingly, the State of Israel has contributed to the denial of Jewish legal rights to the entire country by illegally transferring substantial area of Judea, Samaria and Gaza to the PLO representing a mythical Arabic-speaking Gentle nation called "Palestinians" who falsely pretend to hold the real title of sovereignty over the country.

"Despite all the subversive actions to smother and destroy Jewish legal rights and title of sovereignty to the entire Land of Israel, they still remain in full force by virtue of the Principle of Acquired Rights and the Doctrine of Estoppel that apply in all legal systems of the democratic world." (Dr. Grief's paper can be read in full at www.acpr.org.il.)

Dr. Grief's paper provides the political and legal dynamite that explodes the myth of a Palestinian right to the land of Israel. Not only is there no such biblical right, but there is no legal or political one either. Created out of whole cloth, it is a myth expounded by the Palestinian propaganda machine with great success.

Once again, Israel was taking a place front and center in my thinking. While our biblical understanding of the place and role of Israel was being fine-tuned during these years, there was no place for those views to be fleshed out. And that was frustrating.

The passion was returning—the hole in our heart was being filled once again. But what to do? How do we get the tiger out of the tank? In 1995 we began to see a possibility of a renewed vision taking shape in the future. But more on that after Patty tells you about our Virginia experience from her standpoint.

Patty's Perspective

After living in Virginia for almost twenty-five years, it is difficult to imagine living anywhere else. Before, when I saw the sign "Virginia is for Lovers," I thought it was corny. Now I understand what it means. We had hardly settled when Jim got into the Washington, D.C. National Guard. Later he was sent to Salt Lake City, Utah for ten days. His mother, who lived with us, encouraged me to go with him and I did. While he was in meetings all day, I studied in the mother of all genealogy places—the Mormon archives.

In a way, I owe much to the Mormons for helping me find my place again in the world. I had always thought my line went straight back to John the Baptist, who was really John the Jew who baptized. At the time I grew up, few people I knew talked about what country they had come from, much less if they had ancestors different from them.

The incredible *Roots* movies started something incredible in the lives of everyone. We knew who our grandparents were and that was it. With the exception of Grandmother Ophelia Long knowing that her family had come from the

"Old Country," which to her was Texas, we all just assumed we were from where we were living. Mama did think that the ancestors of her father, Lemuel Lafayette Gilleylen, had come from Wales, although I later found it was Ireland. Daddy used to say that he was "Irish with a little Scotch" in him. I learned much later in life the double entendre in what he was saying

But in Utah and for years now in Virginia, I began to discover some our real roots. Starting from scratch, I found centuries of ancestors, including Catholics, Protestants, and Jews. It is amazing to find that you are related to almost everyone everywhere, and this fact changes one's thinking about all people and all places. Although no one ever finishes genealogy searches, my wall size charts speak to me of hundreds of family names like Calvert (of Maryland), Cantrell (of Jamestown,VA), Ballard, Bealle, Brown, Clark, Cook, Cooper, Cox, Davys, de Dene, Eaton, Edmund, Green, Griffith, Hawte, Haynes, Heath, Howell, Hyatt, Ingersoll, Kirk, Langley, le Strange, Mendenhall, Nash, Parr, Pierson, Roth, Rich, Roemer, Shelving, Smart, Shields, Smith, Thayer, Thompson, Van Gelder, Ward, Watkins Whittington, Wingate, and countless others.

Jim is part Mohawk, yet Tamara, one of his ancestors, was killed by Indians. Aaron Gisnet, a friend from Israel, wrote to us that he now understood why we wanted to be Jews. He said the American Indians were part of the Lost Tribes of Israel. Not only did both of us trace our lines to many pilgrims and early settlers, we found lines to kings and, of course, mostly lesser-knowns and common folks. Somehow, this information was personally healing after the years in Israel, since I was trying to come to terms with who I was and where I was. Strangely, it would help prepare me for personal struggles in the years to come.

Another Miracle Home

God has always worked miracles for us when it comes to houses. As it had been before, when we came to Virginia, we were not sure how we could afford a home. We had seen our house in Illinois miraculously go up in value in only two years, so we had a good sum of money for a down payment. We had sold our rights to the GI bill with that house in Highland Park, so could not get that loan again.

The "greatest real estate agent on the globe," Pat Derwinski, found us a home that had been vacant for two years. We told her we'd buy it without even seeing it inside except to look in all the windows. However, when we went to get a loan, we did not have even half of what it took to qualify and were turned down. "Rejected" was the word. As Yogi Berra would say, "This was deja vu all over again." And again and again.

However, we had strong confidence that God would work it out. So Jim told me to go back to Illinois and sell the house while he stayed here. Matt was entering West Point and was in New York, so Rachel and I returned to Illinois while Jim stayed in Virginia to enroll Sarah in high school and start a church which had no building, no manse, no formal meetings and practically no money.

A few days after I got back to Illinois, I found an Israeli couple who wanted to buy our house. To sweeten the pot, I threw in several paintings with Hebrew letters in them. We still were no closer to getting a loan, but about a week later, I got a telephone call from Mary, a woman whom we had never met, but someone whom Jim had ministered to over the phone several times.

Her son had been in a very serious situation and Jim had been a pastor to her through some tough times—on the phone. After we chatted and shared a few things, she asked me if there was anything to pray about and I told her about the house situation and how we had not been able to get a loan. I did not have the slightest idea that she had any money personally. She then asked me how much we needed and I told her, "About $100,000."

Then she simply replied, "I can get you $100,000 by Monday. I will make you a personal loan and you can set up a repayment schedule with your real estate agent." She was used by God to save us in a real way and start us on a new road. God wanted us in Virginia! We bought the house, and over the years watched its value go up to what Jim had referred to when he gave away the Volvo in Israel, *"Everyone who has left houses or brothers or sisters or father or mother or children or fields, for My name's sake, shall receive a hundredfold..."* (Matthew19:29).

Ronald Reagan

Even Ronald Reagan had a part in our recovery. He was elected President of the United States the year we came to the Washington, D.C. area and he began almost immediately to give honor to all Vietnam Veterans. Once we were invited to a huge event where he took part. When his time came to speak, he started by asking all Vietnam veterans and their families to stand. Then he asked everyone to give them a great hand of appreciation as he thanked us. As we stood, there were few dry eyes watching this great man honor those brave souls who had gotten back so little for giving so much.

Later that evening when we were privileged to go through a line and shake his hand, I took his hand in both of mine and with tears flowing down my face, said, "Mr. Reagan, do you know how much we love you? Thank you for caring. Do you have any idea how much what you did tonight means to us? Thank you so much." Our friends, Valerie and Carlos Moorhead, a Congressman and his wife from California, had invited us and were behind us in the line. They saw and heard everything. When we got through the line, Valerie smiled a big supportive smile, hugged me and

chuckled, "No one ever speaks like that to the President."
And as I told her, "More people should."

Max Jay Mercer

When my Daddy died, it was understandable, because
he was in his sixties and had grandchildren. But the day I got
the phone call from my brother Max's son, saying, "Aunt
Patty, Daddy has gone to heaven," it was probably the greatest blow I had ever known.

"What do you mean," I almost shouted, "he's gone to
heaven? What's the matter with him?"

He said simply, "Daddy passed away, Aunt Patty."

Here was a man who was only forty-six years old, in the
prime of his life, a law professor at Tulane University and
one of the best lawyers Louisiana ever had. He had been Jim
Garrison's personal assistant right out of law school and was
involved in the Clay Shaw case, which pointed to a conspiracy in the assignation of President John F. Kennedy. I have
met lawyers who told me they dreaded getting a case opposite Max. I knew he had won most arguments since he was
a boy. One father said Max had saved his boy from prison
and many people have told me something I knew well,
"There is no one like Max."

Daddy used to make us put on the gloves and box
together, except Max could never hit me. I could hit him as
hard as I was able, but Max only learned a little defense with
me. Although around our house he ruled, treated me like a
baby and controlled my life completely, once he punched
out a guy in high school just for asking permission to ask me
out on a date. He was the brightest, most popular, most interesting, most everything person I knew, and I just could not
believe that Max could die.

Everything about Max was outgoing, fearless and most
of all, alive. He was my big brother, and I was totally devastated by his death. Mama was even worse. I was too bro-

ken to be much help to his wife and children. Once, after I was grown, I accused Mama of loving Max more than all of us, but secretly in my heart, I could see why she might.

Just a few years after Max died, Mama, my beloved sister and older brother all died within a few months of each other. I was the only Mercer left in our immediate family. Death has a sad, final way of contributing to the collateral damage of rejection. In fact, the death of loved ones feels like a huge form of rejection. I asked myself, "Does it ever end?

Healing Times

One thing I can say. With all the trials, troubles and temptations God allows in life, He always comes through by also sending relief, comfort and help in these times of need. It's true that healing is sometimes slow, but it is sure. These years in Virginia have brought great trials, yes, but even greater joys.

All our children are married to responsible, wonderful life partners and are producing incredible grandchildren— eleven so far. We've had hundreds of friends in the Metropolitan D.C. area and through the years of ministry at Christ Church of Arlington. We've planted tomatoes and mowed grass and dealt with Virginia allergies successfully. We've parked at the Train Station in D.C. and taken the train to New York for a concert or Yankee game. We've spent days at Virginia Beach, meditating and walking the beaches with our family. We've dashed back and forth from Virginia to D.C., Maryland, Pennsylvania and West Virginia the way my family used to go to towns 20 minutes from our home. Jim has done pre-marital counseling, married couples, visited their newborn babies and finally baptized them when they grew up - and in some cases performed their weddings. We love the Israeli Embassy and our friends there, as well as those in most of the churches in the area. We've played a fair game of golf at most of the courses within an hour of our home. Our good friend, Dr. Orley Herron, gave me a full grant to get another Masters degree in Management and Human Resources at National Louis University's McLean, Virginia branch. Our cups not only have been but are definitely still running over.

Although a bee sting almost killed me twice, Walter Reed Army Medical Hospital put me on a protocol that restored me with therapy and professional, loving attention. Jim hung in there in the military and was promoted to Brigadier General - and I'm his first lady.

I am privileged to teach painting at the Corcoran College of Art and Design in Washington, D.C., as well as Northern Virginia Community College. The Corcoran sent me for several summers to start the art department at Lord Fairfax Community College near Winchester, Virginia. In 1982, I founded Washington Artworks to teach private art classes and promote visual art exhibitions in the area. A great art collector even took a liking to my paintings and began to buy them for his collection.

Jerry Isley, Director of the Washington Art Group and long time influence in the arts, invited me to write a paper on "Spirituality in the Visual Arts" to present at the 300-year Anniversary of St. Petersburg, Russia at the Hermitage. This started a fire for writing about art that has just begun. Arby's coffee club in our town fills my cup to overflowing with good friends who are there with no agenda. At least I think there no agenda.

One special comfort through all the trials since Israel has been the Bible – the Hebrew Bible. I began in earnest to study it more and more, and as is always the case, God's Word does not return void. It accomplishes what it is sent out to do. At any hour of the day or night, I can be found studying and meditating on the letters of the Hebrew alphabet and writing a bimonthly magazine article, *Hebrew for the Goyim,* for *The Jerusalem Connection.* Of course, if I am reading the Hebrew Bible, I am also reading about Israel, about God's faithfulness to Israel, regardless of Israel's love and faithfulness (or lack thereof) for God. Just as He does with *all* of us saints and sinners, God keeps on keeping on with Israel. Over and over, God keeps saying the same thing, "You are to love my people."

"But Lord, what about the vomit thing? What about the judges and what they said? What about the rabbi who..."

The Lord speaks loudly and clearly to my spirit by His Holy Spirit, "What about you? What about what you have said and done? What about the countless times you have disobeyed or ignored me? What about my love for you in spite of your sin? What about me and what I've done for you? What about my passion?" Of course, God is right.

Recently Jerry, a neighbor, reminded me of what the great Jim Rayburn of Young Life used to say, "Jesus loves you so much that if He carried a billfold, your picture would be in it." It touched me as a high school kid and it touches me now because I know it is true.

So, as I began to recover from the past, I began to feel a strong rekindling of that old love for God's firstborn children, for our elder brothers, the Jews. There is no getting away from it—you have to throw out much of the Bible to turn away from the Jews. Some people have literally done that, making Bibles that include only their favorite and agreed-upon verses, but we cannot. We will not. The next move Jim made was proof of that.

CHAPTER 12

A Second Chance
Leaving the Comfortable Pew

February 1, 2004 was a Sunday that had been coming for a long time—nearly ten years to be exact. The sermon on my last Sunday at Christ Church of Arlington was, *"Following a Hard Example of Jesus."* The text was John 13:1-17. It was about foot washing—an example Jesus says we are to follow. I believe we are to follow it literally, but also we need to determine its meaning for us today. Certainly it's a call to servant leadership—something I had tried to model as pastor of the church I was about to leave.

Parting from our flock was not easy. Patty and I planted the church, and I had been its pastor since November 1982—that's 21 years and two months. That's a long time. Nearly one-third of my life had been spent with the flock of Christ Church of Arlington. They had been a good and generous flock. The elders in the church had been mature and godly men who genuinely sought the mind of Christ in their overseer responsibilities. My Director of Ministries, Tish Williamson, an elementary school teacher in the Alexandria School System, will always be my example of a loyal, faithful and trusted friend and co-worker. She had a written job description, but what it really amounted to was, *"Whatever it takes."* I loved her for that.

Like all sheep, some were healthier than others, some

more willing to follow the shepherd than others, and some more prone to wander than others. But then, all of us were seeking higher ground, regardless of where we started out—including the pastor! Of course, that is because we were under the Great Shepherd who said, *"I will never leave you nor forsake you ... being confident of this, that he who has begun a good work in you will carry it on to completion until the day of Christ Jesus" (Philippians 1:6).*

As one might imagine, after all those years of shepherding this flock, some from the cradle and some to the grave, I had some feelings of possessiveness—even ownership. *Letting go and letting God* was not going to be easy. Yet for some time, I had known that the day would come when I would have to step down as the only pastor many of them had known. If I had to put a date on when this slow growing letting-go seed began to germinate, probably it would be in the late 90's, when Israel stepped back into my life.

New Horizons

The phone rang in my office at the church. "Dr. Hutchens, I am in the Arlington area, and if you have time, I'd like to stop by and tell you about a new venture related to Israel that some Christians are launching." Instantly, the man on the other end of the line had piqued my interest. "We're hoping that you might want to be a part of it," he added.

He gave some other information about how he came to know about me and then asked again if he could meet with me. I gave him directions to the church, and he arrived about twenty minutes later.

An organization from Europe was planning to start a branch of their ministry in the United States. International and non-political, the group drew from Christians of all churches and denominations. Dedication to building bridges between Christians and Jews was their theme. They wanted to serve the Church by helping her to understand God's heart and purposes for Israel and the Jewish people, and at the same time encourage a new appreciation of the Jewish roots of the Christian faith.

Their message for the Church was to accept and love the Jews, to stand in solidarity with them and the State of Israel, and to oppose anti-Semitism wherever it emerged. While praying for the peace of Jerusalem, they wanted to help the Jewish people in practical ways, financially, morally and spiritually. They aspired to unite all Christians in the love for Israel and the Jewish people, believing this to be one of the truest expressions of the Christian spirit. Although evangelism or proselytism, as such, was not a priority, he said, they followed the Apostle Peter's admonition, *"Always be prepared to give an answer to everyone who asks you to give the reason for the hope that you have. But do this with gentleness and respect"* (I Peter 3:15).

Indeed, the message was compelling. It even sounded familiar—I realized that I had heard this before. My mind went back to 1969, twenty-five years before, to the American Institute of Holy Land Studies on Mount Zion in Jerusalem. The founder and president, Dr. G. Douglas Young, had cast that very same vision in almost the same language. The message and the vision were as compelling now as they were then.

I later learned that about that same time, twenty five years before, God in His providence had brought a respected and godly Dutchman under the sway of Dr. Young's vision. The Dutchman returned to Holland; the vision grew and a ministry was born in 1980. Now in 1995, it was being brought to the United States, and I was being invited to be a part of birthing a branch here. The vision had gone full circle—something only God would do. Yes, I would be honored to be a part.

Initially, I served on the Advisory Board with a doctor, a lawyer, a businessman, a radio talk show host and a former congressman. Later, I was invited to serve on the Board of Directors with Dr. Brandt Gustavson who was then the President and Chairman of the Board. At that time he also held the same position with the National Religious Broadcasters. Due to the heavy demands on Brandt's time and energy, he resigned his position in the fall of 2000, recommending to the Board that I be his replacement.

At the invitation of the International President, I accepted the position of President and Chairman of the Board in November of 2000, while continuing the pastorate at Christ Church of Arlington. God in His grace was giving me a second chance to focus on my passion—Israel. Once again God was allowing us to identify with Israel and the Jewish people—this time as *gentile* followers of Jesus. God's covenant of love for His treasured possession does not cease.

Primed and Pumped

After this initial meeting with the representatives of this ministry, my thoughts and studies had renewed direction toward Israel. For years, my pulpit plan had been to preach through one book of the Bible at a time, a discipline that kept me from gravitating only toward subjects I was most interested in. Now that I was becoming more involved with Israel, preaching through a book was even more important to help me avoid the pitfall of personal focus by dealing with the subject at hand. Still, that became more difficult as I saw two emphases continue to grow in my thinking.

One was the abiding fascination with the land of Israel itself and how it was portrayed in the Bible, accompanied by a strong desire to revisit the land. The other, and somewhat related, was the whole issue of "Replacement Theology" or "Supersessionism," which is the notion that Christians and the Church have replaced or superseded the Jews and Israel as the heirs of God's covenant promises.

The revisit to the land came in an unexpected way. Once again the phone rang in my church office. "General Hutchens, your name was given to me by a General friend of yours in the Pentagon," the caller said. Then he told me his name, Gene Bradley, and said, "I have just finished doing an article on the General for the Promise Keepers magazine. During my discussions with him the possibility of his heading a tour of leaders to Israel came up. He said he would do it, but asked me to contact you to see if you would be the Bible teacher. I'd like to come and talk to you about that possibility," he said, and I jumped at it, "Let's talk." When we did meet, I agreed to serve as the Bible teacher/spiritual leader for a tour group to Israel.

This was a very unusual tour of the Holy Land. Leaders who were tops in their field were recruited for this tour. Two 4-star flag officers, a general and an admiral, as well as a 3-star general topped the list. As a 1-star general, I was low man on the totem pole. In the group was a former director of the CIA, producers from *60 Minutes*, an NBA player, a college All-American, two CEOs and two presidents of Fortune 500 companies, a couple of high visibility journalists, an NCAA championship basketball coach, a Hall of Fame baseball player, and on and on.

The purpose of recruiting high profile leaders was to highlight with them the *leadership principles* of Jesus that we encountered on each day's excursion followed by a debriefing at the close of each day. These debriefings were recorded and given to us in notebook form the next morning at breakfast. After the trip, we were to take these principles back to our sphere of influence to try and live them out before those we led. At the same time, we discussed looking for others to recruit to take this same leadership oriented journey, with the goal of multiplying the model by continually passing it on. Certainly this was a worthy goal.

The trip itself was a great success and a highly effective

model with great tried and tested potential. Although the project has not yet reached its potential, Gene Bradley's idea started a model that continues today. This dream of a Leadership Institute teaching the leadership principles of Jesus has been picked up by our ministry and God willing, we want to further develop this concept into an ongoing reality, especially focusing on the leaders of tomorrow—the 18-24 year olds.

Still, for me personally, just to return to the land was an enlivening experience. I must say that my eyes were misty and my heart jumped when our plane finally touched down on this little postage stamp country. Coming in over the Mediterranean, the coastline of Tel Aviv was a wonderful sight. The magnificent drive to Jerusalem brought back delightful memories from the past. And then, Jerusalem— the beloved city—the city Jesus wept over—the city to which He will return. Indeed, I was filled with an inexpressible and glorious joy. Yes, I was home again.

Replacement Theology

In addition to this desire to return and visit the land of Israel, my attention kept turning to a theology that has impacted the very existence of the modern State of Israel, *Replacement Theology,* or *Supersessionism,* as it is commonly called. Clarence H. Wagner Jr. who heads *Bridges for Peace,* an organization founded in 1976 in Israel by the same Dr. G. Douglas Young to implement his vision of establishing relationships of trust, understanding and peace between Jews and Christians, clearly defines Replacement Theology. Wagner rightly argues that Replacement Theology or Supersessionism maintains:

1. Israel (the Jewish people and the land) has been replaced by the Christian Church in the purposes of God, or, more precisely, the Church is the historic

continuation of Israel to the *exclusion* of the former.

2. The Jewish people are now no longer a "chosen people." In fact, they are biblically no different from any group, such as the English, Spanish, or Africans.

3. Apart from repentance, the new birth, and incorporation into the Church, the Jewish people have no future, no hope, and no calling in the plan of God. The same is true for every other nation and group.

4. Since Pentecost of Acts 2, the term "Israel," as found in the Bible, now refers to the Church.

5. The promises, covenants and blessings ascribed to Israel in the Bible have been taken away from the Jews and given to the Church, which has *superseded* them (hence Supersessionism). However, the Jews are still subject to the curses found in the Bible as a result of their rejection of Christ. (Check out this theology: http://www.bridgesforpeace.com/publications/teaching/Article-18.html).

Thus, Supersessionism cancels out all of God's promises to the Jews, *including the land* promises. It denies the continuing validity of what God says is everlasting. For example, to the Supersessionist, what God says in Genesis 17:7-8 is no longer valid.

> *"I will establish my covenant as an **everlasting covenant** between me and you and your descendants after you for the generations to come, to be your God and the God of your descendants after you. The whole land of Canaan, where you are now an alien, I will give as an **everlasting possession** to you and your descendants after you; and I will be their God."*

These promises are no longer valid, says Replacement Theology, because the Jews have not accepted Christ. However, this assertion ignores two important factors. The first is the *everlasting* nature of God's covenants. If God's covenant with Israel is not *everlasting*, as the Bible says it is, how can we be certain that He will keep the promise of *everlasting* life to those who accept Jesus (cf. John 3:16)? Everlasting means everlasting! It means everlasting to both Jews and Christians.

The second factor stems from the thought expressed in the statement, *"I have a real problem with seeing the modern State of Israel, governed by unbelievers, as fulfillment of God's promises. They may be back in the land, but they are not in covenant relationship with God."* This statement fails to recognize God's *planned* sequence of events for the future. For example God says through the Prophet Ezekiel 36:22-32:

> *"Therefore say to the house of Israel, 'This is what the Sovereign LORD says: It is not for your sake, O house of Israel, that I am going to do these things, but for the sake of my holy name, which you have profaned among the nations where you have gone. I will show the holiness of my great name, which has been profaned among the nations, the name you have profaned among them. Then the nations will know that I am the LORD, declares the Sovereign LORD, when I show myself holy through you before their eyes.*
>
> *"For **I will take you out of the nations; I will gather you** from all the countries and **bring you back** into your own land. I will **sprinkle clean water** on you, and you will be clean; **I will cleanse you** from all your impurities and from all your idols. **I will give you a***

new heart and put a new spirit in you; I will remove from you your heart of stone and give you a heart of flesh. And I will put my Spirit in you and move you to follow my decrees and be careful to keep my laws. You will live in the land I gave your forefathers; you will be my people, and *I will be your God. I will save you* from all your uncleanness. ...

"Then you will remember your evil ways and wicked deeds, and you will loathe yourselves for your sins and detestable practices. I want you to know that I am *not doing this for your sake,* declares the Sovereign LORD. Be ashamed and disgraced for your conduct, O house of Israel!"

The chronology of events given here is first to bring the people back, even though in an unbelieving, out-of-covenant state. Second, God will cleanse them from all impurities and give them a new heart. The sequence is first re-gathering, then spiritual restoration. Are we not seeing that re-gathering in our day? Can the restoration be far behind?

Our ministry will continue to address Replacement Theology and Supersessionism as an error in the understanding of the Church regarding Israel and the Jewish people. The stakes are too high to ignore it. The days ahead are critical. Christians must unite together in solidarity with Israel. This does not mean an endorsement of everything the Israeli government does, anymore than we endorse everything our own governments do. It is far from it. But it does mean that we want to bring a Christian perspective to these areas of concern and disagreement.

In our own governments, we are to be a "salt and light" lobby for the truth of God's word in all issues, and specifically, Replacement Theology should be challenged. Further, we must stand with Israel, our elder brother in the faith and the first among equals. We resist those who oppose her, some of whom even oppose her very right to exist.

Bus # 19

Our ministry is attempting to do just that—stand with Israel. As I finished the last chapter of this book, there was en route to the Baltimore Harbor in America, on the high seas, a bombed out bus from Israel—Bus # 19. Eleven people were murdered and 29 wounded in that bus when a homicide/suicide bomber detonated himself on January 29, 2004 in Jerusalem. Our plan for this leftover shell of a bus began by first displaying it just west of the Capitol in Washington, D.C. on May 6, 2004, the National Day of Prayer. Why are we doing this?

First of all we want to encourage support for Israel—to stand in solidarity with the Jewish people against those who would destroy them. We want to continue to raise the public consciousness with respect to the godless brutality and barbarianism of fanatical Islamic Jihadism, terrorism and suicide murderers. We are doing this by providing a biblical context for calling these activities diabolically motivated terrorism. For example, the prayer of Asaph to God pleads:

> *"O God, do not keep silent; be not quiet, O God, be not still. See how Your enemies are astir, how Your foes rear their heads. With cunning they conspire against **Your people**; they plot against **those You cherish**. "Come,"* *they say, "let **us destroy them as a nation, that the name of Israel be remembered no more.**" With one mind they plot together; they form an alliance **against You**. Let them know that You, whose name is the LORD -*

*that You alone are the Most High over all the
earth.*" (Psalm 83:1-5, 18)

It could not be clearer—those who would destroy Israel
as a nation have plotted together and formed an *alliance
against God*, the God and Father of our Lord Jesus. This is
spiritual warfare in its rawest form, and it must be seen and
engaged as such. In addition, we want to provide an opportunity for Christians to join together to pray for the peace of
Jerusalem wherever this bus is seen. If God wills and as
funds are available, we want to proclaim the message that
Bus # 19 represents all across the USA.

Onward Christians Soldiers for Israel!

Going full-time with this new ministry supporting Israel
poses a huge and humbling challenge, yet provides an enormous opportunity. The task is formidable, we don't know
what the future holds and who could even attempt to engage
in such a task? We are Christians and we are for Israel—for
all that God says about Israel. As Christian Zionists, we support the State of Israel as the national, ancestral and God-
promised homeland for the Jews. Our mandate is
summarized by the Apostle Paul in Romans 11:30-31:

> *"Just as you who were at one time disobedi-
> ent to God have now received mercy as a
> result of their disobedience, so they too have
> now become disobedient in order that they
> too may now receive mercy as a result of
> God's mercy to you."*

The mandate is **"to show mercy because of mercy
received,"** and we are carrying out this mandate in several
ways. Did we Christians receive mercy because of Jesus
Christ or not? We, who were "separate from Christ,

excluded from citizenship in Israel and foreigners to the covenants of the promise, without hope and without God in the world" were "brought near through the blood of Christ." Now, according to this passage in Ephesians, we are "no longer foreigners and aliens, but fellow citizens with God's people and members of God's household, built on the foundation of the apostles and prophets"

We have received mercy and been a made a part of the citizenship of Israel. Our lives are forever linked. Now we want to be a part of helping to bring thousands of Jews out of the former Soviet Union back to Israel, including scores of Jewish orphans. Particularly because of the ugly rise of anti-Semitism worldwide, our goal is to see that number grow exponentially as God motivates the hearts of people to help.

In cooperation with The Jerusalem Foundation we have provided financial assistance to the needy and the elderly—for many of the soup kitchens throughout Israel. A little known fact is that Jerusalem is Israel's poorest city, with 40 percent of its teenagers living under the poverty level. We are reaching out to the victims of terror and to the Sanctity of Human Life efforts in Israel as well.

A major goal is to make known God's purposes for Israel and the Jewish people by informing, educating and activating support. We do this primarily through publications, especially our magazine, *The Jerusalem Connection.* To receive a copy or information (1) call 703-707-0014 (2) fax 703 707-9514, (3) write P.O. Box 20295, Washington, DC 20041. Some have asked, "Why are you doing this?" Didn't you learn your lesson? Are you a glutton for punishment? You were "vomited" out of Israel—they don't want you. Let somebody else do it this—get a life!

We have talked and prayed much about the desire to make a difference for Israel. With us, as with many God raises up, there is a deep, spiritual stirring that motivates us to reach out to Israel and the Jewish people. We feel about Israel the way God feels about Israel. His covenant of love for these chosen people, His treasured possession, is still in effect. This is exactly what He says through the Prophet Jeremiah (32:41), *"I will rejoice in doing them good and will assuredly plant them in this land with all my heart and soul."*

There is this same *rejoicing in heart* to be "doing good" for Israel. There are many like us whose hearts God has touched. We have met elderly widows in small towns who have never traveled to Israel, but love the Land and the people of Israel. We have seen both the poor and the rich touched with concern and a desire to be supportive. There are Baptists, Methodists, Presbyterians, Catholics, and Charismatics and Non-denominationalists who stand by Israel. There are "unchurched" and "unreligious" folks who care from the heart. Personally, I feel alive and in sync with the heart of God when I am calling for the support of the Jews in the Land. How does one explain that? I believe it is because God, in His sovereign will, has deeply embedded that desire in our hearts.

So, yes, we are guilty! We are guilty of trying the best we knew at the time to identify with the Jewish people. We are guilty of having a passion for activating God's covenant of love for His treasured possession. We are guilty of loving Israel in a way that only dimly reflects God's eternal love for them. We are guilty of weeping over the Land and people as Jesus did. We may even be guilty of allowing self-centered desires to guide us, but God will be the judge of that. This I do know—God has given us another chance to move and minister in His very heart and soul. It's a call!

As we seek to put legs on that call to Israel and the Jews, it is unconditional and it comes without an agenda. Whether we are personally accepted or rejected is irrelevant. It's not about us. Our family has been blessed beyond our wildest expectations, and God continues to meet all of our needs and most of our wants. If I died today, life has been rich, full of rewards and very exciting. As Rachel once said, "Well, Dad, one thing you can say about our family—we were never bored."

But it is not about our family. It's about being and doing what we believe is God's will at this point in time—and that means standing with Israel because of God's purposes. Some have said we should stop doing this and start trying to convert the Jews. Throughout history there have been plenty of folks trying to do that – zeroing in on Jewish people and when they don't all respond, many have turned against them in horrific ways. In fact one pastor in our area just announced it was his life goal to convert the Jews and Patty's response was that if someone came out publicly and said they wanted to convert all blonde, blue eyed women born in Louisiana - it would make her want to run and hide. Then she added, "I think they should focus on converting the terrorists."

So, would I like to see the Jews accept Jesus? I would like to see the whole world accept Jesus, because of who He is and what He has done for us all. I am personally and deeply satisfied with Jesus. He took a wasted young man, a loser with no past and no future, and He made him all over again—a total about-face, inside and out.

I wish all humanity knew Jesus, but the Scriptures don't really indicate that is going to happen. Those plans and decisions are best left in the hands of a Sovereign and Holy God who does all things according to His own purposes and will. In the meantime, we will show mercy to the Jewish people because of the mercy we have received—and leave the results to God. That's where they rest, anyway.

The task before us poses terrific challenges, yet offers enormous opportunities. One thing we know for sure, we can't do it alone—God never intended we should. We need

Him to accomplish His purposes—He has to enable. But we also need others whose hearts God has touched in a similar way. We know there are many are out there, because we've met them. Perhaps you are one whose heart God has touched regarding Israel, the apple of His eye. Perhaps we can join forces—with a harness binding us together to work toward that which is near to the heart of God. If that is the case, let us hear from you.

And what does the future hold? God alone knows, but I love Adoniram Judson's famous response when questioned by his board after being in Burma for six years with no apparent results. "What are the prospects for the future?" they asked him. Judson replied confidently, *"The future is as bright as the promises of God!"*

Patty's Perspective

Imagine being married to a fearless, moving target—a man who fasts for 40 days at a time and gets up at 4:00 a.m. to pray. Here is a man who has never jumped in at the shallow end of the pool in his entire life—an Airborne-Ranger-Special Forces-Green Beret-Mohawk kind of guy. A man who broke his nose more times than he told me and whose early goal in life was to be the light heavyweight champion of the world. A man who grew-up without a dad and had to have his young wife tell him, "Jim, fathers go in and sit with their kids on the bed at night and tell them stories. You can make them up—just tell them stories."

I can tell you one thing, my mother would have loved being Jim's wife. She was the epitome of an Army XO (executive officer), the one who carries out the commands, the one who gets things done for the Big Guy. She had absolutely no concern about what people said or thought about her. That was her greatest asset. She told me some time after I was grown, "All I wanted to do was help someone do something great."

My mother had deep concern for people less fortunate, especially compassion for blacks in our town who could not even go into the café, much less get a cup of coffee. Think about that in light of her times. Lotta Gilleylen was born in 1898 in Ruth, Mississippi, before women could vote, before most women could go to college (at least in the area she lived in), before most women could get jobs, before women could do almost anything. Because she remembered when women could not vote, she was a vigilant for those rights and always said, "If you have to take me on a stretcher, take me to vote."

People like Mama who are born to make changes seem to be just that—born that way.

I'm not like Mama

I definitely was not born that way. I hate conflict. I would do almost anything for peace, was supersensitive and even weepy from earliest days. Perhaps being raised around alcoholics causes one to be good and try very hard to keep the peace, but I spent half my life worrying about what people thought. I was basically like my Daddy, a man who stayed pretty much to himself and said he was a man of "functions, fishonalities and fish hooks," whatever that meant. He just happened to fall in love with a wannabe mover and shaker. Isn't it always like that—opposites attract? But there is some good in those of us who hate conflict but have strong convictions.

If you put us up against a wall, we usually come through. People who push peace are often able to hang in there for the long haul. We ask questions. We ask a lot of questions. Sometimes we bug people with our questions. We aren't afraid to doubt or wonder about things, about almost everything. And if push comes to shove, people like us just drop to the ground and refuse to budge, because since we don't really want to be out there in the eyes of the world anyway, close to the earth seems like a good place to be.

So again I found myself in a position I had been in before: going along, doing fine and able to envision a few, relatively peaceful years of doing what we were doing, and then, like most normal people, retiring. I kept my '88 LTD Ford in top condition and resisted Jim's efforts every December to get a new car.

When a woman came to the door one day looking for work and asking if I did my own housework, I told her, "Yes, ma'am, I do my own housework, I do my own yard work, I paint my own house and clean my own windows. I vacuum my own floors, wash and iron my own clothes and type my own letters." As I slowed down a moment to gasp for air, she smiled, thanked me and walked away. When I went in the house I felt a little ashamed for being so direct and thought to myself, "Maybe I do need some help." I suppose some of us just like to dig in and stay there, like they say in war - for the duration.

Jews require a Sign

At first, when Jim really got serious about leaving the church, I tried to slow him down with quotes from the Bible. When that didn't do it, I probably unconsciously started to just drag my feet and hope for the best. Finally, I promised to pray about it more, because I thought that if God were talking so loudly to him, I should hear something, too.

One night while sitting in our spa, I looked up into the heavens and prayed, "God, I know it is probably a wicked generation that seeks a sign, but if this is what you want us to do, would you consider giving me some sort of sign?" No more than two to three seconds after the words came out of my mouth, a huge shooting star shot from one side of the sky to the other. It was so shocking, I actually jumped out of the spa and went inside.

Shortly after that, when we were planning a trip to

Buffalo, New York to meet the editor of this manuscript, I somewhat hesitantly approached the Lord again. "God, thank you for the shooting star, and I don't want to push too much, but, I was wondering if you would grant me one more sign? You know—like you did with Gideon and the fleece. You know I really don't want to fly to Buffalo in the winter. You know I'd prefer to go south where it is warm. But, God, if this is what you want us to do, would you give us good weather in Buffalo?"

That prayer went on the back burner, but I started checking the Weather Channel as the week approached. Two or three days before, the forecasters said it might be a good week in New York, and I mentioned my prayer to Jim. On the Friday we flew out of Baltimore, a warm front hit Buffalo. The entire time we were there the weather was a beautiful, balmy spring with everyone basking in beautiful, shirt-sleeve weather. At the same time, a huge ice storm hit the South. Some, or maybe most, might question whether God would listen to a hesitant, questioning, foot-dragging sinner, but this girl took it as a sign.

Get Over it!

On a Sunday morning early in 2004 in Buffalo, we went to hear Dr. Larry Keefauver, who with his wife, Judi, had presented a marriage seminar the day before. That morning he spoke about those things that hinder us from serving God fully, and as they used to say in Louisiana, "Today the preacher stepped on some toes." While he clearly said he was not referring to abuse or long term dysfunction that needs careful, professional care, one thing that stays with me was his admonition to those who shrink back because of hurt, disappointment or rejection by people. He said, "Get over it!"

I think I have reached that point—I'm "over it." Although we are starting over without the comforting walls of the church family around us, a certain peace and confidence about the future have emerged. And it occurred to me that I can say the same thing I said at the beginning, "I have absolutely no clue about what will follow in the years to come."

However, after all these years, I do have great confidence in the One who leads us, who knows it all and wrote it all down in His sovereign plan before the world began, *"I know the plans that I have for you, plans to prosper you and not to harm you, plans to give you a future and a hope"* (Jeremiah 29:11). We can live with that!

EPILOGUE
What's Next?

W hat is next for the Hutchens? What is next for our ministry? Only time will unfold God's plan, but here are matters of immediate concern.

Bus # 19 needs maximum exposure. This is the bombed out bus we brought from Israel to the National Day of Prayer – *Remember Israel Rally*, in Washington, DC. Eleven people were murdered and 50 wounded on this bus on January 29, 2004. This is a solemn reminder to *pray for the peace of Jerusalem*. Ideally, this bus, with its bonding effect between Jews and Christians and its message about godless terrorism will be at a new location in the USA on every weekend for the indefinite future. **If you are interested in having Bus # 19 at your church, synagogue or in your area, please contact our office.** The God has provided this bus for *such a time as this*.

Additionally, I am working on a manuscript on the subject of replacement theology or supersessionism entitled, *The Marcionites Among Us: The Blemish on the Bride,* which will double as a dissertation for final requirements of a Ph.D. This issue is a critical and divisive issue among Christians today – even among Evangelicals. The Church is referred in the Bible as the "Bride of Christ" who will be presented to Jesus spotless and without blemish. Today, however, the Church at large has a huge ugly growth that detracts from her beauty. Pray that this book will address this issue with a timely and winsome word.

Patty is finalizing a manuscript on the Hebrew letters, a compilation of articles she has researched and written about for several years, called *Hebrew for the Goyim.* They have been featured in each issue of ***The Jerusalem Connection*** and as soon as the project is finished, a book will be available to order.

Also, we have launched a new partnership with a group that will enable us to continue efforts for Aliyah – bringing the Jews home to Israel. For that to happen, however, we will need substantial financial help. Please pray with us about how we can work together to be in sync with the heart and soul of God in this matter.

We are asking God to enlarge the audience hearing this message we believe God has given. If you know people who are interested in the ministry or the magazine, ***The Jerusalem Connection***, please either let them know about it, or, send us the information and we will contact them.

And in closing, "The Lord bless you and keep you. The Lord make his face to shine upon you and be gracious unto you. The Lord turn His face toward you and give you peace."

JOIN *THE JERUSALEM CONNECTION* SUBSCRIPTION LIST!

If you want to stay connected to Jerusalem – read The Jerusalem Connection!

The Jerusalem Connection is our premier publication. We often hear about Israel both in secular and religious circles – but how very difficult it is to hear the true biblical perspective from a Christian viewpoint. Each issue of *The Jerusalem Connection* contains International and American news concerning Israel and also includes short Bible teachings on the prophetic times in which we live. We believe that a Christian perspective on what God is doing in Israel can be a vital key into seeing the big picture of God's plan and how He is operating in the world today. Not only that, but to see what God is doing in Israel, brings a sense of urgency and reality to the Church to be used of God as never before. That's right, God is faithful to all His promises, and we see this when we look at the ongoing miracle of Israel today!

We invite you to pray for the peace of Jerusalem and this ministry as we participate together in what God is doing in these momentous days. We also invite you to help financially in our charity projects in Israel and worldwide. Join us as we continue to "show mercy because of mercy received."

Name _____

Address _____

City_____ State _____ Zip _____

Telephone _____ Fax _____

Email _____

YES, I will stand with Israel USA through a contribution in the amount of $_____.

Corporate and individual contributions are permitted. All donations are tax deductible to the extent allowed by law.

Please make checks payable to:
The Jerusalem Connection
PO Box 20295
Washington, DC 20041

Phone: 703-707-0014

BIOGRAPHY

Dr. James M. Hutchens
Chaplain (Brigadier General) US Army (Ret.)
President, Christians for Israel USA

Jim Hutchens, unreservedly calling himself a Christian Zionist, is a man on a mission for Israel – on the forward edge of the battle informing, educating and activating Christian communities on issues related to Israel from Biblical perspectives. He came to faith in Christ as an enlisted paratrooper with the 11st Airborne, graduated from Wheaton College and Dallas Seminary before returning to Vietnam with the famous 173rd Airborne Brigade. His first book, _Beyond Combat_, shares his combat experiences in Vietnam. He later served with the celebrated Green Berets, was Chaplain to Jerusalem's American Institute of Holy Land Studies and Wheaton College, completed a Doctorate at Fuller Seminary and spent two years in Israel before returning to the USA to pastor Christ Church of Arlington. Jim retired from the Army with the rank of Brigadier General.

Pat Mercer Hutchens

Born: Winnfield, Louisiana. MFA, Northwestern University; MS, National Lewis University; BA, Wheaton.

National Scholastic Honor Society. **Teaching**: Northwestern (Art Theory); George Mason (Printmaking/Drawing); Wheaton (Painting); Corcoran College of Art and Design, Washington, DC (Painting); Chesapeake Seminary (Biblical Hebrew); Northern Virginia (Design). Published poet, photographer. Photos for Warner-Fox (Israel). Co-wrote, starred, TV program, Dallas. Work shown: ISART; Israel Art Journals. Chaired, produced "Washington Artworks," Celebrity Art Exhibition, National Museum of American Indian (Smithsonian). Chaired, produced Benefit Art Exhibit for Peruvian Ayacucho Orphans. Solo, juried, invitational exhibitions include Jerusalem, Tel Aviv, Chicago, Los Angeles, New Orleans, New York, St. Petersburg, Russia and Washington, DC. Author of *Hebrew for the Goyim*, bi-monthly article on origins of the alphabet and Hebrew letters.

Breinigsville, PA USA
13 October 2009
225689BV00001B/1/A